Foreign Policy Situations:
American Elite Responses to Variations in Threat, Time, and Surprise

THOMAS L. BREWER
Eastern Michigan University

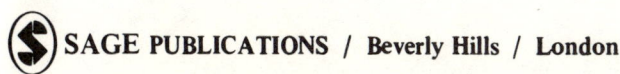

SAGE PUBLICATIONS / Beverly Hills / London

Copyright © 1972 by Sage Publications, Inc.

Printed in the United States of America

All rights reserved. No part of this book may be reproduced
or utilized in any form or by any means, electronic or mechanical,
including photocopying, recording, or by any
information storage and retrieval system, without permission in writing
from the publisher.

For information address:

SAGE PUBLICATIONS, INC.  SAGE PUBLICATIONS LTD
275 South Beverly Drive   St George's House / 44 Hatton Garden
Beverly Hills, California 90212   London E C 1

International Standard Book Number 0-8039-0184-4

Library of Congress Catalog Card No. 72-89159

FIRST PRINTING

CONTENTS

Purpose 5

Variables 7
    Independent Variables: Threat, Time, and Surprise 7
    Dependent Variables: Elites' Process and Output Behavior . . 9

Design and Methods 16
    Cases 16
    Reliability and Validity 19
    Statistical Measures of Effects 21

Findings 23
    Inertia Situations 23
    Reflexive Situations 27
    Deliberative Situations 32
    Routine Situations 37
    Administrative Situations 41
    Total Effects 47

Conclusions 48

Appendix I: Cases Studied 51

Appendix II: Mean Scores for Dependent Variables Across Issue Types According to Threat, Time, and Surprise Interactions . . . 53

Notes 54

References 60

LIST OF FIGURE AND TABLES

Figure 1	Situational Cube Based on Threat, Time, and Surprise	6
Table 1	Variations in Participation Across Cases	11
Table 2	Variations in Cognitive Activity Across Cases	13
Table 3	Variations in Conflict Across Cases	14
Table 4	Variations in Outputs Across Cases	15
Table 5	Distribution of Cases According to Threat, Time, and Surprise Interactions	18
Table 6	Inertia Cases	23
Table 7	Effects of Inertia Situations	24
Table 8	Reflexive Cases	27
Table 9	Effects of Reflexive Situations	28
Table 10	Deliberative Cases	33
Table 11	Effects of Deliberative Situations	34
Table 12	Routine Cases	36
Table 13	Effects of Routine Situations	38
Table 14	Administrative Cases	42
Table 15	Effects of Administrative Situations	44
Table 16	Variance Explained by Threat, Time, and Surprise Interactions . .	46

Foreign Policy Situations: *American Elite Responses to Variations in Threat, Time, and Surprise*

THOMAS L. BREWER
Eastern Michigan University

PURPOSE

While there has been considerable interest in foreign policy makers' behavior in crisis situations, there has been relatively little effort to specify other situational attributes that affect their responses to external events. An important exception is Charles Hermann's (1969a, 1969b, see also 1963, 1972) "situational cube" based on the three variables *threat, decision time,* and *surprise.* The situational cube depicts an eightfold typology of foreign policy situations derived from the eight possible combinations of the two extreme values of each of the three attributes (Figure 1).

Although the effects of such situational attributes have been explored in simulations (Hermann, 1969a, 1972; Robinson et al., 1969), they have not been tested with data from "real world" situations. The purpose of the present paper is to report the findings of a quasi-experimental study (Brewer, 1971, forthcoming) designed, in part, to test the effects of these three situational attributes on the behavior of American foreign policy

---

AUTHOR'S NOTE: *I am indebted to Terry W. Nardin, Charles R. Planck, and Glenn H. Snyder, who shared their thoughts about the study (Brewer, 1971) from which this paper is derived, and to Charles Hermann, who suggested several improvements on a draft version. I, of course, assume full responsibility for its shortcomings. Several excerpts in this paper were taken from James N. Rosenau, editor,* International Politics and Foreign Policy, *revised edition, ©1969, The Free Press.*

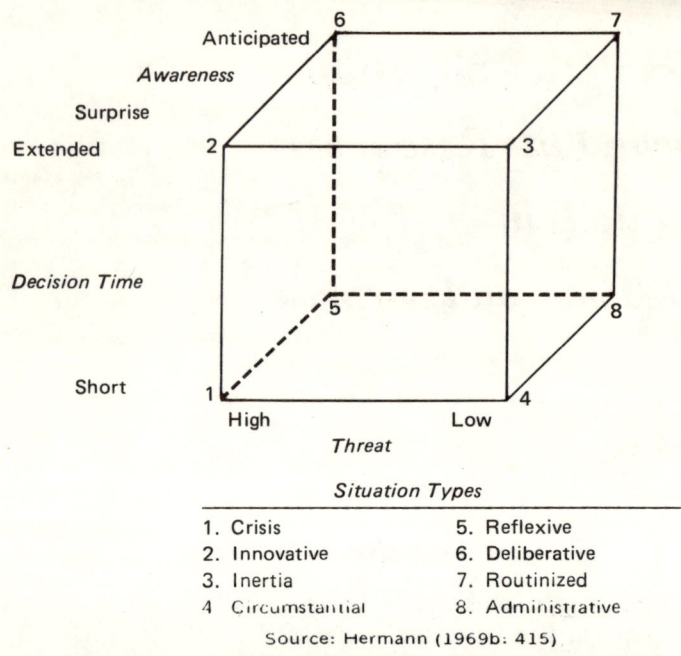

Figure 1: SITUATIONAL CUBE BASED ON THREAT, TIME, AND SURPRISE

elites in 65 cases involving American policy toward European integration or the Atlantic Alliance during the period from 1949 to 1968. In our examination of those findings, we shall be exploring three central questions: *What kinds* of effects do variations in the three situational attributes have on foreign policy behavior? *How strong* are the effects? What are the *strengths and weaknesses* of the situational typology based on them?

The answers to these questions are sought in terms of an analytic framework of American foreign policy-making consisting of "inputs," "process," and "outputs." Accordingly, the 65 situations may be thought of as inputs which activate participants in the foreign policy process. The participants try to influence American policy through interactions among one another and execute outputs in an effort to influence other nations' foreign policies. The content of policy ("outputs") and its consequences ("outcome") are therefore assumed to depend in part on attributes of the foreign policy process and the inputs.[1]

VARIABLES

INDEPENDENT VARIABLES: THREAT, TIME, AND SURPRISE

Hermann, of course, argues that variations in the policy process and the outputs are related to variations in the amount of threat, decision time, and surprise of the inputs. Consequently, we would like to be able to determine for each of the 65 cases each participant's perception of the amount of threat, decision time, and surprise—an enterprise that is clearly not feasible for a large number of cases spread over a 20-year period. We must, therefore, turn to other kinds of data in terms of which we can assign scores to situations in terms of the three variables. The alternative is what Hermann (1969b, 1972) has called properties of situations—i.e., "stimuli independent of perceptions." In other words, situations can be classified by an outside observer according to his own operationalized definitions of the three attributes. While such a strategy is not as satisfying epistemologically as employing direct measures of the participants' perceptions, it is a defensible compromise with what is feasible methodologically.[2] We can now examine the precise manner in which that strategy was applied to each of the three attributes.

In assigning each case a *threat* score, one would ideally determine its exact rank among the 65 cases or even better assign it a score based on an interval level measure of threat. Such precise measures are not feasible, though, and we must rely on a much cruder, but nevertheless serviceable, scale on which cases are assigned a value of either high or low in terms of the threat represented to the above-mentioned American objectives. Hermann (1972: 9 f.) based his operationalized definition of threat on four criteria:

(1) the likelihood "that the source [posing] the threat could execute it without external assistance";
(2) whether the threat would have "blocked all means of reaching the goal";
(3) whether the threat was "accompanied by some action, that is, physical commitment as opposed to merely a verbal warning"; and
(4) whether the threat would have "involved violence, that is, military action."

Each case was assigned a positive or negative score for each of these four criteria and then classified as involving high, moderate, or low threat according to the number of positive scores it was assigned: if all four attributes were present, the case was a high threat situation; if three or two, moderate; if one or none, low.

In the present study, I decided instead to employ another set of criteria in order to have a conception of threat conforming more closely to classical rational decision theory and because the above formulation seemed more appropriate for distinguishing crisis situations from noncrisis situations than for distinguishing among various levels of threat in noncrisis situations.[3] Classical rational decision theory implies that the amount of threat (i.e., payoff) involved in any given situation depends on three factors: the likelihood that a change in the country's value inventory will occur; the distance into the future when it will occur, if it does; and the magnitude of the change that would occur (Edwards, 1954; Taylor, 1965; Tinbergen and Bos, 1962: 25, 90).

While the Hermann conceptualization does take into account—by implication—two of these dimensions (the likelihood of occurrence is implicit in the first three Hermann dimensions and magnitude in the fourth), it neglects the time dimension; that is, it does not provide for any discount for the present value of a future deprivation. Furthermore, the operationalization of the magnitude dimension in terms of the use of violence provides a rather narrow criterion which does not discriminate among noncrisis situations.

The alternative operationalization encompasses all three dimensions and operationalizes them in terms more suited to present purposes. Likelihood is defined in terms of whether or not the threatened objective was certain to be thwarted. Accordingly, if the threat represented a clear, definite and apparently irrevocable (at least in the immediate future) commitment, then it is ranked as high on this dimension—otherwise low. For instance, the French veto of British membership in the Common Market in 1963 represented a certain denial (in the short range, anyway) of the American desire to have Britain "in Europe," while by contrast, the threat that France would no longer participate in the Common Market unless agreements were reached on certain agricultural problems by the end of 1964 did not represent a certain denial of an American objective since the Market's existence was only "in doubt," not certain to be terminated. The time dimension is operationalized in terms of whether the deprivation (if it occurred) would be in more or less than six months.[4] Finally, magnitude is operationalized in terms of the kind of threat—high threat, if it threatens the existence or major program of an organization, or would cost the United States several million dollars; otherwise, low threat. Each case was thus classified as a high or low threat case along each of the three dimensions—likelihood, time, and magnitude. All those cases ranked as high on all three of these dimensions were then given high threat classifications; all others were given low threat classifications. As a result there are 9 cases of high and 56 of low threat.

Decision time depends on both clock time and the complexity of the problem at hand (Robinson, 1968: 514; Robinson and Snyder, 1965: 440 f.; Hermann, 1969a: 29 f.). [5] Clock time refers to the amount of time (in the conventional sense) that will elapse before the situation would significantly change so that any decision would have to be made in less advantageous circumstances. But the amount of effective decision time available is also affected by the complexity of the problem (the number of participants, the number of subtasks to be performed). Consequently, two different dimensions needed to be operationalized. First, whether a given case is low (short) or high (extended) in terms of clock time is based on a judgment as to whether the situation would have changed significantly in less or more than a month. [6] Second, whether or not a case is low or high in complexity is based on whether or not it involved the existence, central structure, or a major program of the organization. In order for a case to be classified as allowing only short decision time, it must be short on both criteria; otherwise, it is classified as an extended decision time case. [7] Eleven short-time and 54 extended-time cases resulted from such an operationalization.

Surprise is operationalized according to whether there were precedents for the situation or whether there was advance notice that the situation might develop. More specifically, the latter was determined on the basis of whether there was an entry in the *New York Times Index* within one month but at least one week before the precipitating event indicating that such an event might happen. Only if neither a precedent nor prior newsworthiness existed is a case coded as being a surprise. The distribution resulting is 6 surprise cases and 59 anticipated cases.

DEPENDENT VARIABLES: ELITES' PROCESS AND OUTPUT BEHAVIOR

To test the effects of these variations in threat, time, and surprise on the American responses to the 65 situations, we need to specify in some detail the process and output variables according to which the elites' behavior has been observed. The process variables can be discussed in terms of: (a) who actively participates in the policy process and how much they participate, (b) their cognitive behavior, and (c) their "political" behavior.

The first set of process attributes concerns the level and scope of participation. The level of participation refers to *how much* active participation there is in any given situation; the *scope* of participation refers to *how many* active participants there are. Variations in both affect the cognitive and "political" dimensions of the process (discussed below) and outputs as well. Most obviously, whether a problem is largely ignored at one extreme or frequently discussed at the other will surely have important consequences on the cognitive and political dimensions of the process and thus on the outputs. For example, the number of consequences of alternatives considered is likely to increase as the level of participation increases. Also the degree of policy continuity in any given situation depends on the number of executive agencies involved: continuity is more likely the fewer the agencies. For, when policy is the domain of only one agency, its interests, constituencies, and world view will tend to promote the status quo; but when it becomes the domain of several agencies, their different interests, constituencies, and world views make it more difficult to maintain policy unchanged. Since environmental changes—i.e., new inputs—are likely to be interpreted differently by different agencies and to be perceived as impinging on agency interests in different ways, new conflicts will occur and therefore new compromises will have to be arranged; and new compromises often constitute changes in policy. Further, the degree of conflict and the amount of diversity in outputs obviously are likely to increase as the number of involved agencies increases. Finally, the importance of the scope of participation is not limited to the number of executive agencies involved; it extends to the number and kinds of participants wherever they are located in the policy process. Thus, we can state rather generally that as the number or type of participants increases, the types and frequency of cognitive tasks and conflict over policy and outputs are all likely to increase.

In view of these considerations, it seemed important to include a variety of types of participants in the analysis. Thus, although Hermann's original formulation focuses on the intrabureaucratic segment of the policy process, my analysis here includes the behavior of extrabureaucratic participants as well. The rationale for such a broadening of the analysis is that the other types of participants serve other types of important functions in the policy process and that their behavior is likely to be differentially affected by situational attributes. Such assumptions about functional and behavioral differences are implicit in the typology of elite participants in Table 1.[8]

The measurements for these and other attributes of the responses to the 65 situations are based on coded entries taken from the *New York Times Index*,[9] which was perused for any act by an American elite participant that was related to any of the 65 cases. All the relevant subject matter headings in the *Index* were searched for the period between the initial and terminal points of each case. For the communications elite category, the

TABLE 1
VARIATIONS IN PARTICIPATION ACROSS CASES
(number of participant acts per case)

Type of Participant	Range
All types[a]	0 – 99
Executive branch	0 – 87
Congressional	0 – 33
Other political	0 – 5
Business-labor	0 – 5
Principled-academic	0 – 3
Communications	0 – 62
Executive agencies	0 – 5

a. Excludes communications category. See page 10.

number of *New York Times* editorials was recorded. For all the other types of participants, each indexed act was recorded on a data sheet as one "participant act" and then coded according to the sets of process and output variables. These participant acts were summed for each variable for each case so the totals thus obtained constitute variable scores for each case. Altogether there were 1,250 participant acts, ranging from 0 for a few cases to 99 for the case involving the French defeat of the European Defense Community in 1954. (The validity and reliability of these data are discussed below on pages 19-21).

While the level and scope of participation are *analytically* distinct, they are *empirically* highly correlated in the present set of cases. Since the two dimensions of participation turned out to vary together so closely (except for the number of executive agencies), the separate indications of the scope of participation were dropped from further analysis to avoid redundancy.[10] In Table 1, where the minimum and maximum case scores for each participant category are displayed, one can easily note that there was considerable variation in the level (and hence the scope) of participation across the 65 cases. The participation level for all types of participants together (except communications) varied from 0 to 99 participant acts; in more specific terms, it varied considerably for the executive branch, congressional, and communications categories but much less for the other categories.

The second set of dependent variables concerns what we shall call the *cognitive* dimension of the policy process, which refers to those kinds of activities directed toward the determination of which course of action is most likely to maximize national objectives. These include, but are not limited to, the thought processes emphasized in the classical model of rational decision-making in its various versions, including game and strategic theory. The cognitive process thus includes specifying and ranking objectives, searching for and defining alternative courses of action, and predicting consequences of considered alternatives. The estimation of other countries' objectives and capabilities as well as one's own are also commonly cited cognitive tasks to be performed in foreign policy decision-making. The importance of feedback (i.e., taking into account the consequences of one's past behavior in the planning of present behavior) has also been emphasized as a central ingredient in the cognitive process.

There are numerous ways in which these types of cognitive tasks are related to attributes of policy outputs. Whether past policy will be continued into the future or changed in any given situation is likely to be affected by how many alternatives to past and present policy are proposed and on how fervently they are advocated. For example, in one of the cases examined in the present study, when the Organization for European Economic Cooperation was not taking sufficient steps toward economic integration in early 1950 to please many American congressmen, the latter strongly advocated alternatives to the administration's policy toward the Europeans, including a proposal to cut off Marshall Plan funds; although the administration did not adopt such stringent alternative measures, it did at least increase its verbal pressure on the Europeans to move more quickly toward a unified regional market. Whether or not a crisis results in the outbreak of war depends, in part, on how thoroughly policy makers have considered the consequences of all possible courses of action, or on the extent to which they have taken into account the objectives and capabilities of the adversary. Or, for another illustration, the frequency with which a country accurately anticipates the effects of its actions is a function of the attentiveness of participants to feedback from previous actions. More generally, the degree to which the actual effects of outputs conform with their intended effects depends on the amount and perspicacity of cognitive activity devoted to the response to a specific situation.

The variables in terms of which variations in cognitive activity have been measured are listed in Table 2. *Attention to U.S. objectives* includes any reference to the goals, purposes, aims, or ends of American policy—in other words, the desired state of affairs. Any indication by an administration official of what the administration has done, is doing, or will do—including references to guidelines and to specific actions—is coded as a *statement of administration policy*. Any indication of the advocacy of a policy or action different from the stated administration policy—whether the alternative is specified or not—is coded as *support for an alternative*.

TABLE 2
VARIATIONS IN COGNITIVE ACTIVITY ACROSS CASES
(number of participant acts per case)

Activity	Range
Statement of administration policy	0 – 9
Support for alternative	0 – 11
Prediction of consequences	0 – 10
Attention to feedback	0 – 3
Attention to U.S. objectives	0 – 17
Attention to U.S. capabilities	0 – 2
Attention to other countries' capabilities	0 – 6
Attention to other countries' objectives	0 – 17

Any attempt to anticipate the effects of administration policy or of any alternative policy is coded as a *prediction of consequences*. *Attention to U.S. capabilities* includes all references to the ability or inability of the United States to attain its goals or to affect another country's behavior. Attention to other countries' objectives and attention to other countries' capabilities are operationalized in the same manner as their counterparts for the United States, except that they of course refer to the objectives and capabilities of the country prompting the threatening situation. Finally, in some theories of foreign policy-making (e.g., Deutsch, 1963), there is an emphasis on feedback as an intellective task; we have therefore included a variable *attention to feedback* which is defined to include all references to the observed consequences of past or current American policies and actions. These, then, are the variables in terms of which we have recorded the amount of cognitive activity in each of the 65 cases. And, as we can readily observe in Table 2, there was a considerable range across the cases in most of the variables. Two exceptions are *attention to feedback* and *attention to other countries' capabilities,* which varied from 0 for such participant acts to, respectively, only 3 and 2. Thus, activity in terms of these two cognitive tasks was at a rather constant, low level across the 65 cases. Otherwise, however, there is substantial variation in cognitive tasks that needs to be explained.

The third set of process variables concerns the participants' domestic *"political"* behavior—that is, their actions and interactions having to do with seeking other participants' support, or granting or denying their own. Hilsman (1959, 1967) has referred to this as the "conflict and consensus-building" process.[11] There are several ways in which such domestic political behavior affects the content of policy (the "outputs"). Thus, delays in reaching a decision, changes in policy, and diversity of outputs are all more likely when conflicts develop because consensus is, by definition, more difficult to obtain and because the formulation and execution of policy depends on achieving a consensus. When conflict arises, more time is needed either to persuade the dissenters "to come along" (perhaps by working out a compromise with them) or to overpower (e.g., outvote) them. A change in policy is more likely, because when conflict occurs it may be necessary for the administration to adopt a compromise between continuing past policy and adopting an alternative offered by a critic. Sometimes there are rather abrupt shifts in policy in response to domestic conflict; for example, in another of the cases considered below, President Johnson has been reported to have ordered the State Department to stop pressing the Multilateral Nuclear Force on the Europeans in 1964 partly in response to domestic criticism (Camps, 1966: 152 f.). Finally, diverse and even contradictory outputs sometimes occur when conflicts among executive agencies are not resolved; in such a situation, each agency may pursue its own independent policy regardless of what "official" policy is. Again, in the case of the MLF for instance, while the State Department avidly worked for European acceptance and participation, the Defense Department, which was never convinced of its military value, did not become an enthusiastic advocate, and, indeed, probably gave the Europeans the impression that it was not a particularly desirable project.

The two indicators of domestic conflict in Table 3 varied substantially from case to case. These two indicators were designed to measure rather direct and explicit conflict and also more subtle forms of conflict. The former was measured by the variable *criticism of the administration,* which includes explicit indications of disagreement with the administration's past or present policies and actions. The latter was measured by *support for alternative,* as defined in the section above. It should be noted that both of these are measures only of conflict in the policy process along anti-administration lines. In fact, of course, conflict frequently occurs along other lines as well—for example, conflicts *within* the administration over which course of action to follow before the administration has adopted a policy.

TABLE 3
VARIATIONS IN CONFLICT ACROSS CASES
(number of participant acts per case)

Indicator	Range
Criticism of administration	0 – 17
Support for alternative	0 – 11

But no way to measure such conflicts could be devised, so we must rely on the partial measures that have been feasible.

The final set of dependent variables consists of *outputs,* which refer to various kinds of externally directed behavior such as issuing threats or promises to foreign actors, deploying missiles, providing economic assistance, or waging war. There are several characteristics of these outputs that students of international politics and foreign policy aspire to explain.[12] There are, consequently, several questions about them worth trying to answer: Are there *any* outputs in a given situation? Is there any response or is there inaction? How *many* outputs are there? Are they numerous or are they rare? Is much said or done, or only a little? What is the *content* of the outputs? Are they favorable and supportive toward the other country or are they unfavorable and nonsupportive? What is the mixture of verbal outputs and actions? Does policy consist of "mere words" or is there action as well? Is policy *coordinated* among the various spokesmen so that there is a single policy or are there several different and perhaps conflicting policies? Do the outputs represent *changes* in policy or a continuation of past policy? What about *timing:* Is policy being formulated and executed promptly in response to changing situations or are there delays?

In Table 4 the types of outputs for which we have data along with the minimum and maximum scores for each type are indicated. There is first a summary measure of the total number of externally directed participant acts by executive branch participants. More specifically, there are two indicators of action. The first indicates whether *any* action was taken and the second the *number* of actions recorded for each case. An action is defined as "any allocation of the nation's resources or any external communication indicating what the nation had done (or would do) about the situation" (Hermann, 1969a: 80 f.).

TABLE 4
VARIATIONS IN OUTPUTS ACROSS CASES
(number per case)

Type of Output	Range
All types	0 – 85
Any action	0 – 1
Number of actions	0 – 8
Consultations	0 – 20
Verbal	0 – 63
Supportive	0 – 25
Nonsupportive	0 – 10
Comments	0 – 32

We are interested in explaining variations in other types of outputs as well, and for this purpose a modified version of the list of interactions used in McClelland's (1968) World Event/Interaction Survey has been adopted. In the initial data gathering process, the externally oriented participant acts were coded according to those categories, but there were so few occurrences in most of the categories that it was decided to collapse them into the broader categories displayed in Table 4. Thus, all reported meetings between American officials and officials of the relevant foreign countries were recorded as *consultations*, whether they occurred in the United States or elsewhere. Also, all participant acts consisting only of verbal behavior were tabulated for each case. But there are, of course, many different types of verbal behavior, ranging from rather dramatic and explicit threats like Dulles' statement that a French defeat for the EDC would prompt an "agonizing reappraisal" of American commitments to Europe, to mild and inconsequential reiterations of previously stated policy, or even refusals to comment. Such a range was reduced to three categories based on the entire McClelland set. *Supportive* outputs include those participant acts (both actions and verbalizations) that represent rather clear American support for the threatening country or countries. It thus comprises the following McClelland categories[13]: "approve" the other country's policy or action; "promise" it support; "grant" it an apology; "reward" it with economic, military, or other assistance; and "agree" with it on some procedural or substantive point. There is also a complementary category for *nonsupportive* outputs—which include participant acts that "reject" the other country's proposal; "accuse" it of acting in an undesirable fashion; "demand" compliance; "warn" it not to take a certain action (without indicating that a sanction will follow); "threaten" it with sanctions; or "reduce a relationship" by withdrawing assistance or terminating some other kind of relationship. Such decisive and explicit responses can be distinguished from the more noncommittal *comments* category, consisting of participant acts in which the participant indicates the situation is favorable or adverse to the United States, or merely refuses to comment.

DESIGN AND METHODS

CASES

These types of variations in the process and output behavior of American elites have been observed in their responses to 65 situations during the 20-year period from 1949 through 1968 when American goals concerning the existence, structure, membership, functions, or major policies of the Western European and North Atlantic organizations were threatened. Such situations were identified from two searches: reading selectively in a large number of surveys of the histories of the Atlantic alliance or European integration and perusing all relevant sections of the *New York Times Index* for each year during the 1949-1968 period.[14]

Three criteria of selection of the cases warrant brief discussion—criteria that, while excluding some important and interesting cases, also served to delimit a coherent and manageable set of cases. First, the goals threatened had to be concerned with European or Atlantic *organizations*. Thus several situations in which American objectives concerning the unity and cooperation among the Atlantic or European countries were threatened were not included because they did not directly concern the organizations. Nor were situations in which the behavior of alliance members were threatening to American objectives not directly concerned with the alliance included; for example, conflicts between the United States and other members over Suez and Algeria were excluded. A second criterion was that the threatening situation had to be the result of an actual or threatened action (or inaction) by a *government;* activities by citizens' groups or opposition parties that may have been regarded as potentially threatening to American goals were consequently excluded. A third criterion was that each case had to have specific, identifiable initial and terminal points; that is, its beginning and ending had to be rather specific and precise—a restriction that was necessary in order to have cutoff points for the observation of participants' behavior.

Selection of the cases on the basis of these criteria yielded the 65 cases listed in Appendix I. They range from major and dramatic events like the French defeat of EDC and de Gaulle's rejection of Polaris missiles and British membership in the Common Market to rather obscure cases like Belgium's demand for more favorable credit terms in the European Payments Union. Further, 34 concerned European organizations; 28, Atlantic organizations; and 3, both. In terms of the country that precipitated the situations, the distribution is as follows: France, 32; Britain, 11; West Germany, 4; Belgium, 1; Iceland, 1; Turkey, 1; and 2 or more countries collectively, 15. The cases are also spread over the 20-year time period and therefore across several American administrations: 19 during the 4 years of the Truman administration from 1949 through 1952; 20 during the 8 Eisenhower years from 1953 through 1960; 9 during the Kennedy years of 1962-1963; and 17 during the Johnson administration from late 1963 through 1968.[15] There is also considerable variation in duration: the shortest, 13 days; and the longest, 399 days.

TABLE 5
DISTRIBUTION OF CASES ACCORDING TO THREAT, TIME, AND SURPRISE INTERACTIONS

Situation Type	Number of Cases	
	n	%
Crisis	0	0
Innovative	0	0
Inertia	6	9
Circumstantial	0	0
Reflexive	3	5
Deliberative	7	11
Routinized	42	65
Administrative	7	11

In Table 5, where the distribution of cases is presented, it is readily apparent that there are three types of situations—crisis, circumstantial, and innovative—for which there are no cases at all. While such a distribution is regrettable, it could not feasibly be avoided. For it will be recalled that the present paper is derived from a larger study (Brewer, 1971; forthcoming b), in which *four* theories about the effects of inputs were tested. Although the set of 65 cases does not provide an entirely satisfying distribution in the Hermann typology, the reader will appreciate the difficulties of finding a set of cases that would provide even distributions for four different typologies. Nevertheless, the uneven distribution of the cases does pose limitations for the findings reported below. In the first place, we obviously cannot test hypotheses about responses in crisis, circumstantial, and innovative situations. Furthermore, we cannot regard the overall correlations for the total effects of the typology as being very conclusive, since such correlational statistics are sensitive to the distribution of cases among the cells of a matrix (here the "situational cube").

While the cases studied are, I think, sufficiently important to deserve study in their own right, the purpose of the study clearly goes beyond understanding these particular cases to the more challenging task of developing a generally applicable theory about the effects of situational variables on American foreign policy-making. For such a purpose, one would, of course, ideally select a large random sample from a carefully defined population of cases and then use tests of statistical significance to determine precisely how confidently he could assume his findings for the sample applied to the population. Clearly, these conditions do not obtain in the present study, so that we are left primarily to our judgment (rather than statistical tests of significance) to determine how confidently we can generalize our findings.

Such judgment must take into account: (1) the population of cases to which we want to generalize; and (2) the representativeness (if not randomness) of the sample. We have already alluded to the restriction of the study to the United States. Given important differences in the political structures, processes, and cultures, one would want to generalize to other countries only very cautiously indeed. Second, we need to specify the time limits. Several considerations suggest the end of the World War II as an appropriate cutoff point—particularly the American position in the world and the size of the foreign affairs bureaucracy. Hence, we shall consider the population to be all American postwar situations.

But is the sample representative of that population of cases, even if it is not a random sample? I think it approximates a representative sample, except for three important restrictions. In the first place, inasmuch as the cases studied here are all part of a larger policy area about which there has been considerable consensus (at least until the past few years) compared with other policy areas, the findings concerning the political dimension of the policy process probably have limited potential for generalization. Second, since these cases involve only situations created by allies, the responses to them are likely to be different in several important respects from what we would expect to find when the threats emanate from neutral or hostile countries. Finally, as we have just noted, there are no cases falling into three of the situation categories. In other respects, though, we have seen that there is a great deal of variety in the kinds of cases.

RELIABILITY AND VALIDITY

The observation of the attitudes and behavior of foreign policy elites poses challenging methodological problems. Much of what they think, say, and do is kept secret. It is difficult and resource-consuming to gain access to them for interviews. Their own accounts are limited and distorted by memory and self-interest. Furthermore, in the present study, there is the problem of needing comparable observations for 65 cases extending over two decades.

As we noted above, the solution adopted in the face of these methodological problems was to use the *New York Times Index* as the source of data. In view of the source of the data, the limitations of the findings of the study must clearly be appreciated. The findings provide only a partial, limited test of the effects of threat, time, and surprise on foreign policy-making behavior. They will of course need to be supplemented by studies employing different types of data and other samples of situations.

All data gathering methods involve problems of reliability and validity, and the present one is surely no exception. But although one is initially inclined to be skeptical indeed of such a procedure, there are persuasive arguments and evidence which substantially alleviate one's uneasiness. They are presented more extensively elsewhere (Brewer, forthcoming a, see also 1971: ch. 2, forthcoming b), but they can be summarized briefly here as follows.

The author coded all the data on which the findings of the study are based, but a research assistant coded a sample of the participant acts so that intercoder reliability tests could be conducted.[16] Such intercoder reliabilities can be tested in several ways. A typical and rather straightforward method is the percentage of agreement between coders for all the items coded. All the variables showed better than 80% agreement, and several, more than 90%. A second indication of reliability is an intraclass correlation coefficient of agreement suggested by Robinson (1957), which is more demanding than the more common product-moment correlation used for such purposes in that it requires *agreement* between the coders, not merely a linear relationship. It is based on *case totals* for each variable, not individual items. The codings for 10 variables were found to have coefficients of agreement of .80 or higher; 3 were between .70 and .79; and 2 were between .60 and .69. (The coefficient varies from −1.0 to +1.0; it is *smaller than a product-moment for the same data.*)

While the *validity* of the data cannot be ascertained so precisely and conclusively, I believe that several considerations should substantially allay the reader's likely sense of uneasiness in this regard. Validity in general refers to the extent to which any given data set in fact measures what it purports to measure. But there are three more specific varieties: construct, predictive, and content. With one marginal exception, intercorrelations among the variables establish that the data have substantial construct validity since the variables within the four sets of dependent variables are generally rather strongly intercorrelated, as one would expect. The exception is in the "political" dimension of the policy process, where direct criticism of the administration and attentiveness to alternatives to administration policy are only weakly—but positively—correlated.

Two kinds of tests established substantial predictive validity—i.e., the ability of our data to predict behavior measured by other data. First, numerous comparisons of the participation levels of several specific participants conformed without exception to what we already "know" about their behavior on the basis of conventional wisdom. For example, the common observation that Dulles was a strong, activist Secretary of State and Eisenhower a weak, passive President in foreign affairs whereas the opposite was true of Rusk and Kennedy is clearly reflected in our data on the participation levels of those principals in our cases. Second, comparisons between our data with statements in more traditional accounts of seven of the cases revealed generally striking confirmation of the predictive validity of the data.

Finally, there is the problem of content (or face) validity which is less amenable to substantiation with evidence, and more a matter of judgment. Content validity can be approached as a problem of sampling. Thus, one asks the question: How representative a sample do we have from the universe of behaviors that we are interested in? In the present study, this question may be more specifically rephrased as follows: How representative a sample of all the American participant acts in the 65 cases has been obtained by coding *New York Times Index* entries? Given that the American foreign policy process is generally rather open and public (except for subversive and intelligence activities and crisis situations—which are not relevant here) and given that the elites obtain much of their information about foreign affairs and communicate with one another and to the public via the "prestige press," and particularly the *Times,* a prestige newspaper seems a defensible data source.[17] Furthermore, there is some evidence of correspondence between the private and public attitudes and behavior of officials (Holsti, 1962, 1967; George, 1955). There is also evidence that the judgments of the importance of events by the *Times* editors at the time of the events correlate rather highly with the retrospective judgments of academic observers (Gamson and Modigliani, 1971: 159-163). Finally, there is evidence that the *Times'* coverage is not only generally more comprehensive than that of other newspapers, it is nevertheless also somewhat typical of that found in major newspapers generally (Gamson and Modigliani, 1971: 157; Cohen, 1967; Brewer, forthcoming a).[18] Again, if the reader does not find these arguments convincing, he is invited to consider them in more detail in Brewer (forthcoming a).

STATISTICAL MEASURES OF EFFECTS

In statistical terms, the Hermann eightfold typology of situations is a second-order interaction model—an *interaction* model because it implies that the *combinations* of the three (dichotomized) variables significantly affect foreign policy-making (rather than the separate effects of each variable added together), and a *second-order* model because it comprises the combinations formed by the variations in three variables (which is one level above first-order interactions involving combinations of two variables). Each possible combination of the three dichotomized variables thus constitutes a separate situation type.

The statistical problem, then, is to determine what kinds of patterns, if any, occur in the elites' behavior, as measured by the four clusters of dependent variables, across issue types. First, each issue type is compared separately with each of the other types in terms of each cluster of dependent variables in order to determine whether the elites' behavior differs between each possible pair of issue types and the direction of the difference—which is accomplished by a straightforward comparison of the mean scores for each issue type for each dependent variable. These comparisons tell us whether the *direction* of the effects of the various issue types is as hypothesized. Second, the total effects of all the issue types together are observed in order to determine the total percentage of variance explained in each of the dependent variables by the entire typology—which is accomplished by the calculation of the correlation ratio (E^2) based on a one-way analysis of variance design. These correlation ratios tell us the *magnitude* or strength of the effects of the entire issue typology.[19]

The tables below also report the levels of *statistical significance*—for the pair-by-pair comparisons of the issue types separately, and for the correlation ratios for the total effects analysis. In a study such as the present one, where there is no random sample drawn from a precisely specified universe of cases, the value and meaning of such significance tests is a moot point. Some argue that a test of significance should be used only in a study employing a random sample. Others (e.g., Blalock, 1960: 269 f.) argue that such a test is almost always worth reporting and that, in the present study, such a test could be construed to have either of two different meanings. (1) If one assumes that we have a sample that approximates a random sample, then it would indicate the (approximate) likelihood that any given finding in the study would also apply to a universe of cases. (2) If one assumes that we are not trying to generalize to a larger population of cases at all but merely trying to ascertain how confident we should be about the findings for this same set of cases, then a test of significance indicates how often any given finding would occur by chance alone. Since there seems to be no consensus on this point, an appropriate convention to follow is to report the values of the tests of significance and thus give the reader an opportunity to observe and interpret them according to his own preference or ignore them altogether if he so prefers; such statistics are, therefore, reported in the following pages. But my own wont is not to attribute any precise meaning to them for the present study, so they are typically ignored or mentioned only incidentally in the verbal discussion of the findings.[20]

Let us turn now to those findings—first in terms of the effects of the situation types individually, and then in terms of their effects collectively.[21]

FINDINGS

INERTIA SITUATIONS

Inertia situations in the Hermann typology are those involving low threat, extended time, and surprise. Among our set of cases, the six listed in Table 6 were coded as such.[22] It has been suggested that such situations

> often lead to decisions not to act or to discussions that never result in a decision. The surprise quality of the situation makes less likely the existence of preparations appropriate for coping with it. Being unexpected, no agency or bureau may see the situation as salient to its own plans. As a result the situation may be discussed by the various offices to which it is referred without the commitment of any agency. A decision is further inhibited by the absence of any sense of urgency. Given the number of policy situations at any given time that pose considerable danger to the objectives of the policy-makers, this type of situation has difficulty being assigned a place on the crowded agenda of men with the authority to commit the state [Hermann, 1969b: 417].

Thus, in terms of the four clusters of dependent variables in this study, we would expect lower scores in inertia situations than in other types of situations. More specifically, the level and scope of participation in inertia

TABLE 6
INERTIA CASES

Britain rejects role in Schuman Plan.
European ad hoc assembly proposes compromise European federation plan.
France opposes nuclear stockpiles and missile deployment in France.
France proposes NATO directorate.
Turkey requests control over nuclear land mines.
France withdraws Mediterranean fleet from NATO.

TABLE 7
EFFECTS OF INERTIA SITUATIONS

	Mean Scores for Inertia Cases Compared with Mean Scores for:			
	Reflexive	Deliberative	Routine	Administrative
A. Participants				
All types[a]	_b	_c	—	—
Executive	—	_c	—	—
Congressional	_c	_b	_d	_b
Other political	+	—	—	+
Business-labor	+	_b	+	—
Principled-academic	=	_b	_d	—
Communications	—	—	—	—
Executive agencies	—	—	+	=
B. Cognitive Activity				
Statement of U.S. policy	_b	_c	—	_b
Support for alternative	—	_c	_d	_b
Prediction of consequences	—	—	—	—
Attention to feedback	+	—	+	—
Attention to U.S. objectives	—	_b	—	—
Attention to U.S. capabilities	=	—	_b	—
Attention to other countries' capabilities	=	—	—	=
Attention to other countries' objectives	_c	_b	—	—
C. Conflict				
Criticism of administration	—	_b	_c	_b
Support for alternatives	—	_c	_d	_b
D. Outputs				
All types	_b	_c	—	—
Any action	_c	_c	—	—
Number of actions	_c	_c	—	—
Consultations	—	—	—	+
Verbal	_b	_b	—	—
Supportive	—	_b	—	—
Nonsupportive	_c	_b	—	—
Comment	—	_c	—	—

a. Excludes communications and executive agencies categories. See page 10.
b. Significant at .10 level.
c. Significant at .05 level.
d. Significant at .01 level.

situations should be below that for other situations; hence the inertia situations should be negatively related to the various measures of participation in comparison with each of the other types of issues.

One would also expect the level of concern reflected in the cognitive dimension of the policy process to be low. The relatively low level of threat would tend to place the situation fairly low in the participants' priority scale; and the element of surprise would tend to leave them without previously considered positions to be espoused publicly.

Just as we would expect low levels of activity in the cognitive dimension of the policy process in inertia situations, so, too, we would expect below-average activity in the political dimension of the process. For the low level of threat would not lead participants to perceive the situations as involving much at stake for their own or others' interest. Furthermore, the element of surprise would mean that whatever interests might be at stake would not necessarily be readily apparent. More specifically, in terms of the two operational indicators of activity in the political process, we would expect negative correlations for direct criticism of the administration and support for alternatives to administration policy.

As explicitly noted in the initial discussion of the inertia situation type, we would, of course, hypothesize a below-average inclination toward positive decision (i.e., action). Operationally, this implies a below-average number of actions taken per case and a relatively low likelihood of any action for a given case of this type. One would expect low scores for other types of outputs as well. In particular, the incidence of acts of a supportive or nonsupportive type (whether verbal or nonverbal) should be low since these types of outputs require some kind of policy position, which is likely to be absent in inertia situations. Further, the incidence of verbal outputs of a rather neutral type (the "comment" category) and of consultations would also be expected to be low in inertia situations since such cases are likely to gain only low priority.

The data of Table 7 show the relative levels of the mean participation scores for inertia cases compared with the means for each of the other types. (A plus sign indicates that the mean score for inertia cases is higher than the mean for the type of case at the head of the column; a minus sign indicates that it is lower. The means themselves are displayed in Appendix II.) In the table, we can note first that the general level of participation in inertia cases is lower than it is for each of the other types; such a finding is evident in the first line, where the mean number of participant acts for all types of participants together is always lower for inertia cases. Further, the negative effects on participation levels generally extend across all types of participants, though the evidence is somewhat mixed for the other political and business-labor categories. Thus, while the hypothesis of generally low participation levels is confirmed, such negative effects are rather uneven, being generally stronger on the governmental participants (executive and congressional) than on participants outside the national governmental institutions. These findings also confirm the expectation of negative effects on the scope of participation, except for the number of executive agencies recorded as being active. For the latter variable, the scope of participation is low in inertia cases in comparison with reflexive and deliberative cases, but not in comparison with routine and administrative cases.

The data in Table 7 also clearly show inertia situations to be negatively correlated with every measure of activity along the intellective dimension of the process, with one exception. The one exception is attention to feedback, which is higher in inertia than in reflexive and routine cases (though not at a statistically significant level). The inertia cases mean scores for both indicators of conflict are also lower than the mean scores for all other types (and usually at the .10 significance level or better).

The findings for outputs are also rather reassuring since, in every comparison in Table 7 except one, the mean score for inertia cases was the low one. Furthermore, the mean number of actions taken in the 6 inertia situations was 0.3, compared with a mean of 0.9 for all 65 cases; and there was some positive action by the administration in only 1 of the 6 inertia cases, compared with an average of approximately 1 out of 3 for all cases. In summary, the participation levels for most types of elites are lower in inertia cases than in any other type; only spokesmen for business and labor interests and political leaders outside the executive and Congress were more active on the average in some kinds of cases than in inertia cases, and then only in two of the four types of cases other than inertia. Since such generally inactive tendencies extend across all types of elite participants, there is not much scope in the types of participants in inertia cases. Nor are there a large number of executive agencies actively involved in inertia cases, at least in comparison with reflexive and deliberative cases; it does tend to be higher, though, than in routine cases, and about the same as in administrative cases. Such inert tendencies are also evident in the cognitive and political dimensions of the policy process; for both indicators of the latter and nearly every type of the former, the participants are the least active in inertia cases. And, finally, the inclination to direct behavior toward other countries is the weakest in inertia situations for every form of outputs except one; consultations are more likely in inertia than in administrative cases.

Such a tendency toward inertia was evident in the American response to President de Gaulle's proposal for a NATO directorate of France, Britain, and the United States in 1958.[23] The situation was initiated in mid-September of that year when de Gaulle sent a message in which he suggested that the organization be restructured in such a way as to give France, Britain, and the United States a predominant role and advocated the extension of the geographic coverage of the treaty. Not until more than a month later was there a response from the administration, and then only in the form of a letter from President Eisenhower in which he merely indicated opposition to the proposal and a willingness to explore "the matter in appropriate ways."[24] Over the next several weeks, Secretary Dulles and Undersecretary Murphy held two meetings with the French and British ambassadors in Washington, and Secretary Dulles made a brief reference to the issue during a press conference—but only to indicate doubt that de Gaulle had proposed a "super-directorate." Nor was there evidence of much attention devoted to the issue by elites outside the administration. Thus, although there was not complete inertia, the American response was quite delayed and cursory. There were surely strong tendencies toward inertia.

REFLEXIVE SITUATIONS

Such uniformly confirming evidence was not obtained for reflexive situations—that is, those characterized by high threat, short decision time, and anticipation; yet on balance the evidence is confirmatory for this situation type, too. Only three of the present cases fell into this category, and they are briefly described in Table 8.

Hermann (1969b: 418) has described the likely reaction to such situations thus:

> With decision time at a premium, no elaborate search routines or consultations are possible to disclose methods for coping with the situation.... Because they will experience a serious threat to their goals if it does develop, the policy-makers probably produce a contingency plan in the period before the situation emerges. Once the situation appears, minor alterations may be made in the

TABLE 8
REFLEXIVE CASES

Organization for European Economic Cooperation approves interim report noting lack of progress in trade liberalization but not advocating a more concerted effort.

Britain fails to announce support for European federation.

Britain rejects proposed division of ERP funds in OEEC.

TABLE 9
EFFECTS OF REFLEXIVE SITUATIONS

	Mean Scores for Reflexive Cases Compared with Mean Scores for:			
	Inertia	Deliberative	Routine	Administrative
A. Participants				
All types[a]	+[b]	−[b]	+	−
Executive	+	−[b]	+	+
Congressional	+[c]	−	+	−
Other political	−	−[b]	−[d]	−
Business-labor	−	−[c]	−[b]	−
Principled-academic	=	−[b]	−[d]	−
Communications	+	−	+	−
Executive agencies	+	+	+[b]	+
B. Cognitive Activity				
Statement of U.S. policy	+[b]	−	+	+
Support for alternative	+	−	+	−
Prediction of consequences	+	−	+	+
Attention to feedback	−	−[b]	−	−
Attention to U.S. objectives	+	−	+	−
Attention to U.S. capabilities	=	−	−[b]	−
Attention to other countries' capabilities	=	−	−[b]	−
Attention to other countries' objectives	+[c]	−	+	+
C. Conflict				
Criticism of administration	+	−	−	−
Support for alternatives	+	−	+	−
D. Outputs				
All types	+[b]	−	+	+
Any action	+[c]	+	+[b]	+
Number of actions	+[c]	−[b]	+[b]	−
Consultations	+	−	−	+
Verbal	+[b]	−	+	−
Supportive	+	−	+	+
Nonsupportive	+[c]	−	+	−
Comments	+	−[b]	−	−

a. Excludes communications and executive agencies categories. See page 10.
b. Significant at .10 level.
c. Significant at .05 level.
d. Significant at .01 level.

proposed plan, but time pressures deny decision-makers the chance to consider major alternatives. In fact, the knowledge that they have already considered the problem may lead policy-makers to an almost reflexive response.

Our expectations about the levels of activity along the cognitive dimension of the process are, therefore, rather clear; they should tend to be negatively affected. But what we should expect of participation and conflict levels is not so clear. As to the level and scope of participation, high threat would lead to an expectation of high participation levels because of the high priority and stakes. Further, anticipation would tend to lead to high participation levels since participants' positions would have been previously determined. On the other hand, the element of short decision time would make it difficult for participants to assert their views. But such an impact would probably be unevenly distributed across participants: nonexecutive branch participants would be more restricted than executive branch participants. On balance, then, we would expect the level of participation of executive branch participants in reflexive situations to be the same as or slightly above that that for other types of situations—since the counterbalancing effects of the short decision time would not affect them as much as other participants. The level of participation among other types of participants would tend to be low in reflexive cases compared with inertia and deliberative situations; but there are no particular expectations in comparison with routine and administrative cases.

So as to the scope of participation, we would anticipate in view of the above discussion that activity would tend to be limited to the executive branch, though the extent to which this would be true would depend on the balance of the conflicting forces on the nonexecutive participants. The scope of participation within the executive branch is rather difficult to predict, though the following line of reasoning seems plausible: Since all agencies would presumably share some anticipation of the situation, each would have an equal opportunity to voice its position once the situation developed. Indeed, the impact of the short decision time could well be to encourage agencies to promote their positions publicly to ensure that they be heard before an authoritative decision is reached.

The data of Table 9 generally confirm these hypotheses. The level of participation among executive branch participants, which we have hypothesized to be above the level for other situations, is in fact higher than it is in three of the other issue types, though lower than it is in deliberative situations. As to the scope of participation within the executive branch, the final line indicates that reflexive situations are somewhat higher than other types. The remaining participant comparisons in Table 9 indicate that the behavior of other types of participants outside the executive branch is also usually as hypothesized since all except congressmen and communications elites have low scores in comparison with both inertia and deliberative cases. And similarly, all except congressmen and communications elites also have low scores in reflexive cases compared with routine and administrative cases (no hypotheses were formulated for these comparisons).

As to the cognitive dimension of the process, we have already noted that our general hypothesis is that, in reflexive situations, activity should be low, though not necessarily any lower than in inertia and routine cases. The evidence in Table 9 is mixed, but confirmative on one key point: Reflexive situations do have a negative impact on the level of attentiveness to alternative policies, in comparison with deliberate and administrative cases. The table contains additional corroborating evidence in that the scores for attention to feedback from previous American behavior, attention to American capabilities, and attention to other countries' capabilities are typically low compared with other types of cases.

The data on domestic conflict are also somewhat mixed, though they typically conform with a prediction of negative effects for reflexive situations. Such a finding is to be expected on the basis of the following reasoning: Whenever participant activity does occur, it is likely to be concentrated in the executive branch (as we have already seen it is); and to the extent that participants outside the executive branch are activated, their behavior is likely to be focused on outputs rather than domestic political interactions, since there is not likely to be sufficient time available for the latter to develop or have any effects on outputs by executive participants. Whatever conflicts are engendered are likely to develop within the executive branch and not be revealed in public anti-administration statements.

The data on outputs seem to fit quite nicely into a pattern that would be expected in reflexive situations. In the first place, the implication of the Hermann discussion above is that the likelihood of action in reflexive cases is high compared with other types of cases. And, indeed, in all 3 of the reflexive cases there was some kind of action—which is well above the probability of 0.38 for all 65 cases. The other measure of action taken (i.e., the *number* of actions taken in each case) is also above the average score for all cases—1.3 in reflexive cases and 0.9 in all cases—although it is lower than the scores for deliberative and administrative cases. Moreover, these slight differences in the effects on the two measures of action are in accord with a reflexive response pattern. For the fact that there is less strong positive impact on the number of actions taken than on the probability of any action indicates that once policy makers have executed a previously devised course of action, they do not tend to follow-up the initial action with additional improvised, ad hoc commitments of resources—an interpretation consistent with the description of reflexive situations by Hermann above.

The findings for the other types of outputs listed in Table 9 also tend to fit a reflexive output pattern, though not perfectly. All types of outputs are higher in reflexive than in inertia cases, and lower than in deliberative cases. The former is to be expected, since there is a widespread lack of activity in inertia cases; the latter is also to be expected, since deliberative cases would tend to evoke the more verbal kinds of outputs, which would be channelled more in the intellective realm than in the political, since behavior that is critical of the administration in one way or another is relatively infrequent. Although some attention is given to alternatives to administration policy, it is less than in deliberative or administrative situations. Among the elites in the executive branch, there is a strong inclination to take some kind of action—more so than in any of the other types of situations; but there is less likelihood of numerous actions and of other types of externally oriented behavior.

Briefly, then, in reflexive situations, there is a high probability that some kind of commitment of resources will be made—the highest among the five types of issues in fact—but somewhat less likelihood that other types of outputs, including more numerous actions and the more verbal forms, will be forthcoming. And, while participation tends to be relatively frequent among members of the administration and the foreign affairs bureaucracy, it is relatively rare among most of the other types of participants; consequently, there is also relatively little criticism of the administration in evidence. Finally, the amount of cognitive activity is moderately low and somewhat concentrated in statements of American objectives and policy and other statements, mostly by administration spokesmen, that provide miscellaneous information to the elites and the public about the issue. The cognitive dimension of the policy process is therefore rather dominated by explication of the administration's policy.

These tendencies are particularly evident in one of the three cases classified as involving high threat, short decision time, and anticipation—namely, the one initiated by the British in October 1951 when the newly installed Conservative government failed to indicate its support for European integration, including the recently proposed European army. The planning for such an army was under way, but the French government was demanding British support as a precondition for French participation.

Although there was no immediate American reaction to the British position, several weeks later the administration did present a relatively elaborate and specific proposal, including a commitment to help finance the project, if the British would agree to four forms of support, if not membership: training European pilots, providing blueprints of technological advances in weaponry, participating in joint maneuvers, and planning and deploying forces in cooperation with the Europeans. There were also some high-level American-British consultations, but little else in the way of outputs. Nor was there much active participation by congressional or other actors, though Senator Russell did demand that the administration press Britain to become a member.

DELIBERATIVE SITUATIONS

The third type of situation considered here is characterized by high threat, extended time, and anticipation—a combination of attributes found in the 7 cases of Table 10. Such cases are likely to induce a process labelled "deliberative" by Hermann (1969b: 419), who has described it in these terms:

> High threat increases the probability that the situation receives careful attention, but unlike a crisis, the deliberations are not limited to a small group of the highest-ranking officials. Consideration of the problem occurs at different levels and in different agencies. The time available for discussion both prior to the actual appearance of the situation (as a result of anticipation) and after it emerges (as a result of extended decision time) can lead to organizational difficulties. Many groups in and out of government may become committed to a particular method of handling the problem.... Deliberative situations increase the likelihood of hard bargaining between groups with alternative proposals.

Clearly, then, we would hypothesize that deliberative cases would evoke high levels of participation, in comparison with other types of situations, across all categories of participants and thus a broad scope of participation as well, both within and outside the executive branch. As the name and the quotation from Hermann above suggest, we would also predict high levels of activity in the cognitive process. The participants are also expected to be highly engaged in the policy process politically so that the two indicators of domestic conflict should be high relative to the other types of cases. Finally, the combined attributes of high threat, extended decision time, and anticipation would tend to yield above-average levels of outputs.

TABLE 10
DELIBERATIVE CASES

Britain and France oppose German role in European rearmament.
Germany exhausts credits in EPU.
France proposes Pleven Plan.
France rejects EDC.
Iceland requests removal of U.S. bases.
"The Seven" sign European Free Trade Association treaty.
EEC decides to raise tariffs on poultry.

Such expectations are generally confirmed. Most of the mean participation-level scores for deliberative situations are the highest for any situation type. Such an effect is reflected in the great preponderance of plus signs in Table 11. One obvious exception to such effects is the congressional participation level, which is lower in deliberative than in administrative cases—a finding that is initially rather perplexing, since one would expect congressional participants to be especially active in deliberative situations, particularly in comparison with administrative cases. Further examination of the data, though, explains the problem. Two unusual cases—both of the administrative type discussed below—had levels of congressional participation that were extremely high and thus pushed up the mean score for that type of issue. The scope of participation clearly extends into the nongovernmental sphere, as predicted, even allowing for the aberration in the congressional score. And the scope of executive agency activity within the government is also high relative to three of the four other types of issues. The hypothesized effects of deliberative cases on the scope of participation are therefore confirmed on both counts.

The data of Table 11 are also in accord with the prediction of high levels of activity in the cognitive process; deliberative situations are positively correlated with all of the indicators of cognitive activity, in comparison with other types. The two reversals in comparison with administrative issues are a result of the two cases which were just mentioned and which will be discussed in more detail below. Thus, in terms of this hypothesized central characteristic of deliberative situations, the evidence from our 65 cases is conclusively favorable, with only minor exceptions.

The evidence on conflict as presented in Table 11 is mixed. It indicates that there is considerable attention devoted to alternatives to administration policy, except in comparison with administrative cases, which again show a reversal of the expected relationship. The pattern is similar for

TABLE 11
EFFECTS OF DELIBERATIVE SITUATIONS

	Mean Scores for Deliberative Cases Compared with Mean Scores for:			
	Inertia	Reflexive	Routine	Administrative
A. Participants				
All types[a]	+c	+b	+b	+b
Executive	+c	+b	+b	+
Congressional	+b	+	+	−
Other political	+	+b	+	+
Business-labor	+b	+c	+b	+
Principled-academic	+b	+b	+	+
Communications	+	+	+	+
Executive agencies	+	−	+	+
B. Cognitive Activity				
Statement of U.S. policy	+c	+	+b	+
Support for alternative	+c	+	+	−
Prediction of consequences	+	+	+	+
Attention to feedback	+	+b	+	+
Attention to U.S. objectives	+b	+	+	−
Attention to U.S. capabilities	+	+	+	+
Attention to other countries' capabilities	+	+	+	+
Attention to other countries' objectives	+	+	+	+
C. Conflict				
Criticism of administration	+b	+	=	−
Support for alternatives	+c	+	+	−
D. Outputs				
All types	+c	+	+b	+b
Any action	+c	−	+d	+
Number of actions	+c	+b	+c	+
Consultations	+	+	+	+b
Verbal	+b	+	+b	+
Supportive	+b	+	+b	+b
Nonsupportive	+b	+	+b	−
Comments	+c	+b	+b	+

a. Excludes communications and executive agencies categories. See page 10.

b. Significant at .10 level.

c. Significant at .05 level.

d. Significant at .01 level.

more direct criticism of the administration, except that the mean scores are equal for deliberative and routine cases.

Both indicators of positive action verify an expectation of high levels of outputs. In 6 of the 7 deliberative situations, some kind of positive action was taken—a proportion well above the figure of 1 in 3 for all 65 cases, and the second highest score among the 5 types. Such situations ranked first in terms of the number of actions taken with a mean score of 2.8 actions recorded, compared with 0.9 for all cases. These strong effects on the probability of positive action are reflected in the statistically significant positive effects for those two variables in Table 11. Nor is the one exception—reflexive situations—surprising since, as we have seen, the likelihood of some kind of action in reflexive situations has been hypothesized as quite high. All of the other output data in that table indicate positive effects in deliberative situations, without exception. Thus the tendency toward high levels of outputs in deliberative situations extends to consultations with foreign governments and to various forms of verbal behavior.

In sum, that combination of threat, time, and surprise labelled deliberative by Hermann is likely to evoke widespread and quite active involvement in the policy process across all types of elites. There is likely to be more intensive and extensive involvement in deliberative cases than in any other type. Furthermore, there is likely to be more examination of alternative courses of action and their consequences, and the consequences of past policy, and more attention to other countries' desires and capabilities, than in any other type of situation; the deliberation includes high levels of attention to numerous aspects of foreign policy analysis. Such unusually comprehensive consideration of foreign policy problems spills over to some extent into conflict with the administration. It also tends to coincide with unusually numerous outputs—more numerous in fact than in all other types of situations (except for the likelihood of any action, which is lower than in reflexive situations)—but predominantly of a verbal type as opposed to commitments of resources.

Among the seven cases classified as deliberative, one of the early ones which concerned German rearmament best illustrates such behavior. In mid-September 1950, the foreign ministers of both France and Britain announced their governments' opposition to a major German role in the rearmament of Western Europe, as called for by the United States. During the course of the next few weeks, there was widespread and active participation—including numerous public announcements and reports from several executive agencies: the Economic Cooperation Administration, which administered the ERP; the State Department; the newly created

TABLE 12
ROUTINE CASES

OEEC proposes only partial reduction of import quotas.
Britain opposes role of NATO Military Committee Secretary-General advocated by United States.
Belgium objects to its credit terms in EPU.
German opposition to Ruhr settlement delays Schuman plan.
Germany rejects French proposal for structure of European army.
Britain rejects Council of Europe advocacy of European federation.
Britain announces intention to reduce troop commitment to NATO.
Belgium and the Netherlands issue report critical of NATO military strategy.
Italy and Germany propose mandatory consultation within NATO.
France proposes European free trade area.
Germany fails to budget support for U.S. NATO troops.
European Atomic Energy Community rejects U.S. inspection proposal.
Greece breaks military ties with Turkey and removes troops from NATO command in Turkey.
France announces preference for national cooperation rather than integration.
France proposes revision of NATO to make it less integrated.
France opposes integrated air defense system.
France proposes European confederation with new institutions under national control.
France proposes revision of NATO to include non-European areas and asserts that French defense is primarily national in character.
France proposes reform of NATO.
France asserts French forces and Franco-German solidarity are keys to French security.
France vetoes British membership in European Economic Community.
France rejects U.S. offer of Polaris submarines.
France asserts need to be its "own master" and to build independent nuclear force.
France withdraws naval forces from NATO Atlantic fleet.
France announces EEC "may disappear" if agreement is not reached on agricultural policies.
France rejects NATO responsibility for defense of France and disposition of French forces.
France rejects Europe in Atlantic partnership.
France rejects European federation, advocates confederation.
France withdraws officers from NATO Mediterranean and English Channel naval commands.
France advocates "independent" Europe.
France announces it will "cease to participate" in EEC if agricultural markets are not established in accord with previous agreements.
Britain proposes alternative to American MLF plan.
France rejects U.S. "hegemony," advocates changes in NATO.
France boycotts EEC.
France rejects U.S. proposal for nuclear planning committee in NATO.
France opposes integrated defense after 1969.
France proposes alternative to NATO.
France announces it will withdraw from NATO military planning and assert its sovereignty.
France vetoes British membership in EEC.
Germany announces reduction in financial support for U.S. NATO troops.
France vetoes British membership in EEC.
Germany and France advocate Europeanwide tariff reduction but without British membership in EEC.

Defense Department; the Army and Navy; and the Office of the American High Commissioner in Germany. The latter sponsored a public opinion poll to determine German public sentiment on the issue of German rearmament. There was also active participation among several congressmen—including a group that went to Europe on a "study tour" of the situation and Senator Cooper, who called for the sending of additional American troops to Europe and the establishment of a unified command structure—and among Republican leaders—such as Harold Stassen, who pledged his party's support for American military aid for European rearmament—and, finally, among businessmen, through their spokesmen in the National Association of Manufacturers and the Chamber of Commerce.

ROUTINE SITUATIONS

Routine situations, according to Hermann, are those ranking low on the dimensions of threat and surprise but allowing extended time for decision. As previously mentioned, this category contains by far the largest number of cases. A listing of the 42 such cases in Table 12 reveals considerable heterogeneity among them.[25] Just as there is substantial variation within this category in terms of the situational attributes, so too there is presumably considerable variation in the responses to those situations. For while

> these situations tend to be dealt with by policy-makers at the lower and middle levels of the organization . . . the decision process follows one of two general patterns. In the first pattern decision-makers treat the problem in the same manner as they have treated previous situations of the same genus. Execution of the recommended course of action follows prompt agreement, unless temporary delays develop because policy-makers, whose approval is required, are engaged in more urgent business. If the situation lacks precedent or becomes the pawn in an interagency dispute, it follows the second pattern. Under these circumstances it may never come to a decision or may lie fallow until personnel change [Hermann, 1969b: 419].

Yet, in spite of these two different patterns among routine cases, there is still reason to expect generally low levels of activity in terms of all of our clusters of dependent variables. For, regardless of which of the two patterns obtains for any given routine case, it will be handled for the most part at the lower levels of the bureaucracy. On occasion, however, such issues may spill over into the more public arenas of the policy process, in which case there would be some activity on the part of extrabureaucratic participants.[26] To the extent that the particular issue was recurrent, it

TABLE 13
EFFECTS OF ROUTINE SITUATIONS

	Mean Scores for Routine Cases Compared with Mean Scores for:			
	Inertia	Reflexive	Deliberative	Administrative
A. Participants				
All types[a]	+	—	—[b]	—
Executive	+	—	—[b]	+
Congressional	+[d]	—	—	—
Other political	+	+[d]	—	+
Business-labor	—	+[b]	—[b]	—
Principled-academic	+[d]	+[d]	—	—
Communications	+	—	—	—
Executive agencies	—	—[b]	—	—
B. Cognitive Activity				
Statement of U.S. policy	+	—	—[b]	—
Support for alternative	+[d]	—	—	—
Prediction of consequences	+	—	—	+
Attention to feedback	—	+	—	—
Attention to U.S. objectives	+	—	—	—
Attention to U.S. capabilities	+[b]	+[b]	—	—
Attention to other countries' capabilities	+	+[b]	—	+
Attention to other countries' objectives	+	=	—	—
C. Conflict				
Criticism of administration	+[c]	+	=	—
Support for alternatives	+[d]	—	—	—
D. Outputs				
All types	+	—	—[b]	—
Any action	+	—[b]	—[d]	+
Number of actions	+	—[b]	—[c]	—
Consultations	+	+	—	+[d]
Verbal	+	—	—[b]	—
Supportive	+	—	—[b]	—
Nonsupportive	+	—	—[b]	—
Comments	+	+	—[b]	—

a. Excludes communications and executive agencies categories. See page 10.
b. Significant at .10 level.
c. Significant at .05 level.
d. Significant at .01 level.

would give extraburaucratic participants pause about the ability of the bureaucracy to handle the issue adequately and give them opportunities to participate in their resolution. On the other hand, the low threat dimension would tend to push these routine cases down the list of issues over which participants are willing to expend their scarce resources.

For a variety of reasons, one would anticipate a generally low level of activity in the cognitive process in routine situations. The existence of precedents would encourage only minimal consideration of alternatives. Furthermore, advocates of change can be expected to conserve their intellective energies on the assumption that only extraordinary circumstances will stimulate interest in change. Again, however, routine issues can be expected to receive as much as or more attention than inertia issues.

For the political dimension of the process, our predictions rest on three considerations. As in the case of participation levels, there are factors operating in opposite directions. The recurrence of such threatening situations should tend to undermine confidence in the prevailing policy or policy-makers responsible for formulating and executing it. In other words, as similar threatening situations begin to accumulate, one would assume that past and current management of affairs would come under increasing citicism. Yet, on the other hand, the low level of threat would tend to discourage any prolonged or severe conflict. Further, the frequent existence of prior situations of a similar nature might encourage nonbureaucratic actors to leave them to the disposal of the bureaucrats since, presumably, guidelines for their disposition already exist. On balance, then, we would expect the level of conflict to be relatively low, though not especially low and not lower than it is in inertia cases.

Finally, low levels of outputs are hypothesized for routine cases, except in comparison with inertia cases, since the outputs that do occur would tend to be carried out at the lower levels of the government, generally out of the public view, and hence frequently not recorded in our data source.

The data of Table 13 concerning the scope and level of participation are consistent with the prediction of low scores. First, we can observe that for every category for which we have data, the mean score for routine cases is lower than the mean score for deliberative cases. Second, we can note that all but two of the scores for routine cases are below those for administrative cases. One of the exceptions is rather perplexing; the other is not. The higher score for executive branch participants in routine than administrative issues is clearly contrary to expectations. But the finding that political elites outside the national governmental institutions would tend to be more active in routine than in administrative issues is not so perplexing since they would, of course, be expected to be generally inactive in administrative cases. As compared with reflexive cases, most of the mean scores for routine cases are lower, though there are three conspicuous exceptions for the other political, business-labor, and principled-academic categories. For these three groups, who are outside the national governmental institutions, one should not be surprised at such a pattern, however, since, as we indicated above, recurrent issues do occasionally spill over into the more public arenas and since, by contrast, reflexive situations are not likely to give such participants much opportunity to voice their concerns. Finally, routine issues do tend to evoke more participation than do inertia cases, as we have hypothesized. There is, then, in Table 13 substantial support for the hypothesized effects of routine issues on the scope and level of participation, though there is the one important aberration in which participation by executive branch actors is higher then in administrative cases.

As to the cognitive dimension of the policy process, the data of Table 13 reveal few exceptions to the predicted pattern. The few exceptions that do occur are once again in the comparisons with administrative cases and with reflexive cases. But, on balance, the findings are rather strongly confirmative. The findings as to conflict, though, are rather mixed. In terms of support for alternatives to the administration's handling of the issues, conflict is low in routine cases, except in comparison with inertia situations. The pattern is not so simple in terms of more direct criticism of the administration; for there the mean score for routine cases is lower than the score for administrative cases, the same as the score for deliberative cases, and higher than the scores for both reflexive and inertia cases.

The pattern in the findings for outputs is more clear. There was some kind of administration action recorded in 31% of the routine cases, as compared with 38% for all 65 cases. In terms of the number of actions taken, routine cases showed an average of 0.5 per case, compared with 0.9 for all 65 cases. The other types of outputs also tended to be negatively affected by routine issues, except in comparison with inertia cases, as we hypothesized.

There is, therefore, a pattern in the elites' behavior in the 42 routine cases examined here. For the most part, they are relatively quiescent, though not as much as in the inertia cases analyzed above; they tend to leave such matters to lower- and middle-level bureaucrats, whose actions and interactions are usually outside the purview of our observational data. The generally low scores for routine cases extend to both intellective and political dimensions of the process. There are nevertheless some occasions on which the elites are rather more responsive since the political leaders outside Congress and the administration, as well as business, labor, principled interest group and academic participants, tend to be somewhat more active in routine than in reflexive cases. There is then some evidence of variability in the responses, as we noted there would be in the initial description of routine situations above; specifically, two different patterns were anticipated. In one, agreement among bureaucrats is reached rather quickly, and policy is executed on the basis of previous responses to precedents. In the other, the lack of precedents or the occurrence of conflict leads to inaction—at least temporarily.[27]

Among the 42 routine cases of the present study, there are two that fit these two patterns rather well and can therefore be used to illustrate them. The first refers to a German plan, supported by France, to establish a Europeanwide free trade area, including Britain, that would involve substantial reductions of tariffs among the European countries but no reductions of external tariffs and no British membership in the Common Market. The American response was quick and direct. The same day the European plan was announced, an administration spokesman denounced it and said it appeared to violate rules of the General Agreement on Tariffs and Trade (GATT), and within a week the American Embassy in Bonn delivered a note to the West German government condemning the plan. Finally, an administration report on trade policy reasserted American opposition two months later. There was thus no evidence of extensive active involvement by upper-level administration officials, nor by elites outside the executive branch.

The second type of routine situation can be illustrated by reference to a report to the 1957 NATO Parliamentary Conference issued by Belgian and Dutch representatives, who criticized the prevailing NATO strategy of reliance on (American-controlled) nuclear weapons. Over the next several weeks, most of the American response emanated from representatives of the military, though Secretary of State Dulles also responded. But there was some difference in the responses from the spokesmen from the two agencies: Whereas the military emphasized that the Europeans' report was not an accurate statement of existing policy, Dulles proposed even greater emphasis on nuclear weapons. There was also some spillover into the more public domain, and some conflict of views as well, when a report sponsored by the Rockefeller Brothers Fund suggested increasing the conventional ground troops in Europe and putting nuclear weapons under European control in order to decrease reliance on American air power.

ADMINISTRATIVE SITUATIONS

The final category of situation types has been labelled administrative by

Hermann (1969b: 420) since situations involving a combination of low threat, short decision time, and anticipation will presumably "engage middle level officials of foreign policy organizations." The 7 cases listed in Table 14 were so classified from the 65 studied here. More elaborately, Hermann (1969b: 430) has described these situations as being characterized by the following:

> Efforts to seek out new information about the situation are limited by the short decision time and by the relatively low priority of low threat situations in gaining access to the government's facilities for search. In a fashion similar to reflexive decisions, the treatment of an administrative decision depends on the extent to which policy-makers have taken advantage of their expectation that the situation is likely to occur. If they anticipate that the situation will involve minimal threat, policy-makers may be reluctant to invest much time in the preparation of a possible response. On the other hand, when a low threat situation materializes they have less of a felt need for some kind of action than do the participants in a reflexive situation. Hence, those engaged in an administrative decision are unlikely to act at all unless they are confident that the proposed response is appropriate to the situation.

Thus, in comparison with reflexive and deliberative issues, we can hypothesize low levels of participation for executive participants—since it is only the high-level officials, for the most part, whose behavior is recorded in our data source; we can also anticipate low levels of participation for other participant types in terms of these two comparisons. But we would expect higher levels of participation in administrative cases than in inertia cases. The expectation in comparison with routine cases is that administrative cases would tend to be the same or higher (as we noted in the discussion of routine cases).

The description of administrative situations taken from Hermann clearly leads to a prediction of negative effects on the variables indicating

TABLE 14
ADMINISTRATIVE CASES

Spain asks to be included in European Recovery Program.

Britain objects to proposed European Payments Union.

OEEC annual report proposes only partial integration plan.

Germany indicates reluctance to join Council of Europe.

Britain rejects role in EDC.

Britain rejects French-German-U.S. accord on ownership of Ruhr steel companies thereby threatening Schuman Plan.

France proposes European arms pool.

cognitive activity in comparison with deliberative cases, but positive effects in comparison with inertia cases. The relative scores in comparison with reflexive and routine cases are more difficult to predict since they too are expected to have fairly low levels of cognitive activity.

For the third set of data—those indicating conflict in the policy process—we predict low to moderate scores which would be higher than those for inertia situations, lower than those for reflexive and deliberative situations, and about the same as those for routine situations.

Finally, as to outputs, we predict that administrative situations would be low in comparison with reflexive and deliberative but high in comparison with inertia and routine situations.

The findings reported in Table 15 are not always in accord with such expectations, but they do nevertheless offer some verification. The mean scores for administrative issues are generally higher than those for inertia cases and lower than those for deliberative cases. But among the numerous exceptions to our expectations that occur elsewhere in the table, the most glaring one is that congressional activity in administrative cases is higher than in deliberative cases—a rather troublesome finding encountered above. A closer look at the particular administrative cases helps to explain the latter divergence from expectations. There were two administrative cases in which congressional actors were particularly active; in all the other administrative cases they tended to be rather quiescent, as predicted. The two aberrant cases occurred during the early months of 1950 when the American objective of European economic cooperation was threatened. One was prompted by British opposition to the proposed European Payments Union and the other by an OEEC report that advocated trade liberalization measures far short of those expected and desired by the administration and Congress. And both cases occurred at a time when the European Recovery Program appropriations bill was before Congress. Thus both involved an issue that was already quite salient for congressmen and other elites who were following the congressional processing of the bill quite closely. It is not surprising, therefore, that congressional and some nongovernmental elites were particularly responsive to these threats.

As the cognitive variables data of Table 15 indicate, the mean scores for administrative cases do tend to be higher than those for inertia situations and lower than those for deliberative situations, as predicted. Yet, there are two exceptions to such a relationship with deliberative cases, and one of them, as we observed in the discussion of deliberative cases above, is support for alternatives, which is a particularly disturbing reversal. Again, then, we are compelled to look more closely at the specific cases involved. And, as was the case for participation levels, the two cases mentioned

TABLE 1b
EFFECTS OF ADMINISTRATIVE SITUATIONS

	Mean Scores for Administrative Cases Compared with Mean Scores for:			
	Inertia	Reflexive	Deliberative	Routine
A. Participants				
All types[a]	+	+	−[b]	+
Executive	+	−	−	−
Congressional	+[b]	+	+	+
Other political	−	+	−	−
Business-labor	+	+	−	+
Principled-academic	+	+	−	+
Communications	+	+	−	+
Executive agencies	=	−	−	+
B. Cognitive Activity				
Statement of U.S. policy	+[b]	−	−	+
Support for alternative	+[b]	+	+	+
Prediction of consequences	+	−	−	−
Attention to feedback	+	+	−	+
Attention to U.S. objectives	+	+	+	+
Attention to U.S. capabilities	+	+	−	+
Attention to other countries' capabilities	=	+	−	−
Attention to other countries' objectives	+	−	−	+
C. Conflict				
Criticism of administration	+[b]	+	+	+
Support for alternatives	+[b]	+	+	+
D. Outputs				
All types	+	−	−[b]	+
Any action	+	−	−	−
Number of actions	+	+	−	+
Consultations	−	−	−[b]	−[d]
Verbal	+	+	−	+
Supportive	+	−	−[b]	+
Nonsupportive	+	+	−	+
Comments	+	+	−	+

a. Excludes communications and executive agencies categories. See page 10.

b. Significant at .10 level.

c. Significant at .05 level.

d. Significant at .01 level.

above are responsible for the aberration. Except for those two cases, there was a rather low level of cognitive activity in the policy process.

But the findings on conflict levels in Table 15 show that both indicators of conflict reached their highest means in administrative cases; in other words, on the average, conflict was greater in administrative cases than in any other type. Most surprisingly, both indicators show higher mean levels of conflict for administrative than for deliberative cases. Once again, closer examination of the data reveals that the same two administrative cases are the ones responsible for the surprisingly high scores. The high conflict scores were the result of congressional demands that the administration take a more firm stand with the Europeans and pressure them to move faster toward liberalized trade policies.

The data of Table 15 for all types of outputs together fit the predicted pattern perfectly (though they do not reach the .05 significance level). More specifically, in only 2 of the 7 cases was there some kind of action—a proportion of 0.29 that is somewhat below the average of 0.38 for all 65 cases. On the other hand, in terms of the number of actions taken, administrative situations were above average—1.4 compared with 0.9. But the two administrative cases that contributed most to the other scores discussed above also were responsible for whatever action did occur. In othe words, there were enough actions taken in those two cases to push up the mean for this category of situations even though there was no action in 5 of the 7 cases.

Before drawing a summary description of elite reactions to administrative situations, we need to reiterate that the several deviations from the hypothesized effects that were found could be accounted for by 2 cases with extremely high scores on several variables. In both of those cases, the fact that the issues were already highly salient matters before Congress and the public seems to have been more of a determinant of nonexecutive elite responses than the issue attributes of threat, time, and surprise. Except for those two extreme cases, the behavior of the elites outside the executive branch conformed to the low profile expected of them, so that among these other administrative cases there was a pronounced tendency to eschew intensive cognitive and political efforts and leave matters in the hands of the administration and the bureaucrats, who tended to handle them relatively inconspicuously since the scope and level of participation among executive branch elites and agencies were moderately low. The frequency of outputs was in the middle range—lower than in deliberative and reflexive issues, but higher than in inertia and routine issues.

In the case involving West Germany's membership in the Council of Europe, such patterns of behavior are particularly evident. The case arose

TABLE 10
VARIANCE EXPLAINED BY THREAT, TIME, AND SURPRISE INTERACTIONS

	Percentage of Variance Explained
A. Participants	
All types[a]	8
Executive	10
Congressional	15[c]
Other political	3
Business-labor	25[d]
Principled-academic	4
Communications	14[b]
Executive agencies	6
B. Cognitive Activity	
Statement of U.S. policy	8
Support for alternative	8
Prediction of consequences	4
Attention to feedback	2
Attention to U.S. objectives	4
Attention to U.S. capabilities	7
Attention to other countries' capabilities	12[b]
Attention to other countries' objectives	7
C. Conflict	
Criticism of administration	7
Support for alternative	8
D. Outputs	
All types	11
Number of actions	26[e]
Consultations	7
Verbal	11
Supportive	20[d]
Nonsupportive	13[b]
Comments	6

a. Excludes communications and executive agencies categories. See page 10.

b. Significant at .10 level.

c. Significant at .05 level.

d. Significant at .01 level.

e. Significant at .001 level.

when Chancellor Adenauer announced in March 1950 that Germany did not want membership in that organization unless certain conditions were met. Secretary of State Acheson replied for the administration and said the United States still supported German membership but without the German conditions. Three weeks later, the American High Commissioner in Germany assured the Germans that the United States would not try to control the German representative in the council. Two weeks after that the German cabinet approved membership, and the Parliament finalized the decision the following month. The affair was handled by the administration, in other words, without active involvement by other American elites.

TOTAL EFFECTS

In addition to the need to determine the direction of the effects of each of the situational types, there is the important task of determining the explanatory power of all the situation types together—a task to which we shall now turn.[28]

The correlation ratios indicating how much variance in the level and scope of *participation* across the 65 cases is explained by the threat-time-surprise model are displayed in Table 16. (It should be recalled that these correlations should be regarded as tentative in view of the distribution of cases.) In Table 16, we can observe first that there is a considerable range—from 3% for other political participants to 25% for business-labor representatives. Executive and congressional participants are in between, with 10% and 15%, respectively, of the variance in their participation levels accounted for; the figures for principled-academic and communications participants are 4% and 14%; finally, only 6% of the variance in the number of executive agencies recorded as being active is explained. In sum, while the typology has only moderate and rather uneven explanatory power for who actively participates and how much, it nevertheless accounts for 10% or more of the variance in the level of participation in four categories of elite participants: executive, congressional, business-labor, and communications.[29]

The effects on the *cognitive* process tend to be somewhat less than this; for the nine intellective variables listed in Table 16, the mean percentage of variance explained is 8%. Beyond this summary measure, we can note that the effects are particularly weak on the consideration of consequences of present behavior and of past behavior (i.e., feedback).[30] Further, of all the intellective variables, only one has 10% or more of its variance explained—namely, attention to other countries' capabilities.

The data in Table 16 indicate a comparable magnitude of effects on the indicators of domestic *conflict*. Variations in the interactions of threat, time, and surprise account for 7% of the variance in direct criticism of the administration and 8% in support for alternatives to administration policy. Neither indicator, therefore, reaches the 10% figure.

The effects on outputs, though, are substantially stronger. In particular, *a full one-fourth (26%) of the variance in the number of actions taken is explained* (significant at .001). Furthermore, a phi-square measure of correlation was .21 (significant at .001) for the variable *any action*.[31] While none of the other correlation ratios for the output variables in Table 16 is as high as 26%, they are nevertheless rather substantial; all but two are over 10%. The effects on outputs, in sum, are much greater than they are on the other three clusters of variables.

CONCLUSIONS

What can we conclude more generally about the Hermann typology on the basis of the findings of this paper? There are, I think, six points to be made. The first is that most of the hypothesized effects of the individual situation types are confirmed; indeed, for the overwhelming majority of the predicted effects for all five types, the data conform to our expectations. In particular, there is strong evidence of delay and only limited reaction in inertia situations; the elite participants tend to be less active in every respect in those situations than in any other type. And, in reflexive situations, there is evidence of strong tendencies in the administration to react with some kind of commitment of resources as well as evidence that elites outside the administration do not typically become very active. By contrast, for deliberative cases, there is substantial evidence of considerable active involvement in the policy process on the part of all types of elites, who subject the administration's policy to extensive deliberation and criticism. Among the routine cases, there is evidence of the more limited, quiet, and frequently delayed diplomatic responses concentrated at the lower levels of the foreign affairs bureaucracy than are expected. Finally, the administrative cases provide some evidence of more responsive, higher-level, and more public diplomacy that is somewhat concentrated in the executive branch.

Since the clarity of such patterns was not the same for all five types of situations, however, a second observation is in order—namely, that although the effects of inertia, reflexive, and deliberative situations were rather clear and predictable, the effects of the routine and administrative cases were not. While the data for administrative cases frequently fall into a pattern indicating a predominance of executive branch participants in the policy process, they also show signs of deviation from such a pattern, particularly extensive congressional engagement. But, as we saw, nearly all the deviant behavior can be accounted for by two extreme and unusual cases. Any final judgment on the effects of administrative cases will have to be deferred until we have the results of additional studies. Also, more research will have to be done to clarify the differences in the two different patterns expected in routine situations.

Third, though, we can conclude on the basis of our findings that the explanatory power of the Hermann typology is rather impressive in terms of its ability to account for variations in the tendency to take action since the correlation ratio for the variable indicating the number of actions taken shows that about one-fourth of the total variance can be explained by the interactions of threat, time, and surprise. Furthermore, we saw that the pattern in both indicators of action was nearly always that predicted for each situation type, and high explanatory power extends to most other types of outputs as well. We also observed that the predicted effects on the scope and level of participation by executive branch participants were nearly always confirmed and that one-tenth of the variance in their participation level was explained. In other words, the Hermann typology does, in fact, contribute considerably to our understanding of the participation levels and outputs of executive branch participants—and these are precisely the kinds of effects emphasized in the Hermann formulation.

Fourth, for the other types of dependent variables under examination, where Hermann has been explicit about the predicted effects, the data also generally confirm the hypotheses. This is particularly true of the cognitive process in deliberative situations where rather strong positive effects were recorded.

Fifth, the findings are not otherwise so positive. For many of the hypotheses that could be derived from the Hermann formulation, the data did not fall in convincing patterns. The effects are often weak, and sometimes contradictory. Thus, the amount of variance explained in the cognitive and conflict variables is, as we have just seen, generally rather low.

Sixth, there are several conceptual problems that need further consideration—among them the conceptual basis for the operationalization of threat. In particular, it seems more satisfying conceptually to base the threat variable on the three-dimensional rational decision theory notion of payoff or expected gain (loss), as we have done in the present paper, rather than the four Hermann criteria, which include the use of force. While an expectation of the occurrence of violence may provide one important distinction between crisis and noncrisis situations, it does not enable us to distinguish among noncrisis situations very well. Nor are the remaining Hermann criteria sufficient for this purpose.

Another conceptual problem lies in the distinction between participants' perceptions of threat, decision time, and surprise on the one hand, and those variables as "properties of situations" on the other. Relying on the latter by way of observers' classifications of cases may help us circumvent the difficulty of taking measurements on the former in other than true experimental conditions. But in the process of solving the methodological problem, we are likely to create an epistemological one. For we must either assume that observer classifications are close approximations of participants' perceptions, as we have done in this paper, or we must dispense with a phenomenological explanation of the link between the situation attributes and the policy makers' responses. One cannot develop a phenomenological explanation of the *participants' behavior* on the basis of the *observers' perceptions,* unless the latter are assumed to be indirect measures of the *participants' perceptions.*

Regardless, the classification of cases—whether according to the participants' perceptions or the observers' classifications—poses considerable obstacles. The problem with the former of course is that they are very difficult to collect data on; and the data that might be available for this purpose would not be comparable across cases or participants. On the other hand, if we rely on observer classifications, we must necessarily use rather arbitrary cutoff points for dichotomizing the variables. Such a problem is not peculiar to the Hermann typology; it is a common problem in social science research generally, since one necessarily often operationalizes "real world" interval- and ordinal-level phenomena as dichotomies. Yet, the problem does need further thought in any refinement of the Hermann typology.

But there is sufficient merit in the typology to warrant the effort. While the typology needs to be applied to other sets of data, I think the evidence and elaborations of the present paper demonstrate encouraging improvement in our understanding of the foreign policy-making behavior of American elites.

APPENDIX I
CASES STUDIED
(includes year in which precipitating event occurred)

Organization for European Economic Cooperation approves interim report noting lack of progress in trade liberalization but not advocating more concerted effort (1949)
Spain asks to be included in European Recovery Program (1949)
Britain rejects proposed division of ERP funds in OEEC (1949)
OEEC proposes only partial reduction of import quotas (1949)
Britain objects to proposed European Payments Union (1949)
Britain opposes role of NATO Military Committee Secretary-General advocated by United States (1949)
OEEC annual report proposes partial integration plan (1950)
Germany indicates reluctance to join Council of Europe (1950)
Britain rejects role in Schuman Plan (1950)
Belgium objects to its credit terms in EPU (1950)
Britain and France oppose German role in European rearmament (1950)
Germany exhausts credits in EPU (1950)
France proposes Pleven Plan (1950)
German opposition to Ruhr settlement delays Schuman Plan negotiations (1950)
Britain rejects role in EDC (1951)
Britain rejects French-German-U.S. accord on ownership of Ruhr steel companies thereby threatening Schuman Plan (1951)
Germany rejects French proposal for structure of European army (1951)
Britain rejects Council of Europe advocacy of European federation (1951)
Britain fails to announce support for European federation (1951)
European ad hoc Assembly proposes compromise European federation plan (1953)
France rejects EDC (1954)
France proposes European arms pool (1955)
Iceland requests removal of U.S. bases (1956)
Britain announces intention to reduce troop committment to NATO (1957)
Belgium and the Netherlands issue report critical of NATO military strategy (1957)
Italy and Germany propose mandatory consultation within NATO (1957)
France proposes European free trade area (1958)
Germany fails to budget support for U.S. NATO troops (1958)
European Atomic Energy Community rejects U.S. inspection proposal (1958)
Greece breaks military ties with Turkey and removes troops from NATO command in Turkey (1958)
France opposes nuclear stockpiles and missile deployment in France (1958)
France proposes NATO directorate (1958)
France withdraws Mediterranean fleet from NATO (1959)

France announces preference for national cooperation rather than integration (1959)
"The Seven" sign European Free Trade Association treaty (1959)
France proposes revision of NATO to make it less integrated (1959)
France opposes integrated air defense system (1959)
France proposes European confederation with new institutions under national control (1960)
France proposes revision of NATO to include non-European areas and asserts that French defense is primarily national in character (1960)
France proposes reform of NATO (1961)
France asserts French forces and Franco-German solidarity are keys to French security (1962)
France vetoes British membership in European Economic Community (1963)
France rejects U.S. offer of Polaris submarines (1963)
France asserts need to be its "own master" and to build independent nuclear force (1963)
EEC decides to raise tariffs on poultry (1963)
France withdraws naval forces from NATO Atlantic fleet (1963)
France announces EEC may "disappear" if agreement not reached on agricultural policies (1963)
France rejects NATO responsibility for defense of France and disposition of French forces (1963)
France rejects Europe in Atlantic partnership (1964)
France rejects European federation, advocates confederation (1964)
France withdraws officers from NATO Mediterranean and English Channel naval commands (1964)
France advocates "independent" Europe (1964)
France announces it will "cease to participate" in EEC if agricultural markets are not established in accord with previous agreements (1964)
Britain proposes alternative to American MLF plan (1964)
France rejects U.S. "hegemony," advocates changes in NATO (1964)
France boycotts EEC (1965)
France rejects U.S. proposal for nuclear planning committee in NATO (1965)
France opposes integrated defense after 1969 (1965)
France proposes alternative to NATO (1965)
France announces it will withdraw from NATO military planning and assert its sovereignty over French soil (1966)
Turkey requests control over nuclear land mines (1967)
France vetoes British membership in EEC (1967)
Germany announces reduction in financial support for U.S. NATO troops (1967)
France vetoes British membership in EEC (1968)
Germany and France advocate Europeanwide tariff reduction but without British membership in EEC (1968)

APPENDIX II
MEAN SCORES FOR DEPENDENT VARIABLES ACROSS ISSUE TYPES ACCORDING TO THREAT, TIME, AND SURPRISE INTERACTIONS

	Inertia	Reflexive	Deliberative	Routine	Administrative
Participation					
All types[a]	8.83	16.66	34.42	15.26	23.57
Executive	7.66	13.66	29.57	12.09	12.00
Congressional	0.50	3.00	3.38	2.14	9.71
Other political	0.50	0.00	1.00	0.64	0.42
Business-labor	0.16	0.00	1.28	0.04	1.00
Principled-academic	0.00	0.00	0.42	0.33	0.42
Communications	4.16	4.66	14.57	4.21	5.00
Executive agencies	2.00	3.00	2.57	1.80	2.00
Intellective Activity					
Statement of U.S. policy	0.66	3.00	3.42	1.21	2.71
Support for alternative	0.16	1.33	2.28	1.21	3.28
Prediction of consequences	0.33	1.33	1.71	0.76	0.71
Attention to feedback	0.16	0.00	0.28	0.11	0.28
Attention to U.S. objectives	1.83	3.66	4.57	2.78	5.00
Attention to U.S. capabilities	0.00	0.00	0.28	0.04	0.14
Attention to other countries' capabilities	2.00	4.66	5.14	2.28	3.85
Conflict					
Criticism of administration	0.16	0.66	1.14	1.14	4.28
Support for alternative	0.16	1.33	2.28	1.21	3.28
Outputs					
All types	7.00	13.66	28.71	11.28	12.00
Any action[b]	0.16	1.00	0.85	0.30	0.28
Number of actions	0.33	1.33	2.85	0.47	1.41
Consultations	2.16	3.00	6.57	3.52	0.85
Verbal	4.50	9.33	19.42	7.28	9.71
Supportive	0.83	2.00	6.28	1.30	1.42
Nonsupportive	0.50	1.33	3.14	0.80	2.42
Comments	2.50	3.66	9.00	4.09	4.28

a. Excludes communications and executive agencies categories. See page 10.
b. Refers to percentage of cases rather than mean.

NOTES

1. For discussions of distinctions and relationships among "process," "outputs," and "outcomes," see Easton (1965), Ranney (1968), and Van Dyke (1968).

2. The epistemological problem is that the theory rests on phenomenological explanations of the participants' behavior; that is, their behavior is explained in terms of *their perceptions*. In order to continue to rely on such phenomenological explanations, we must assume that there is at least a rough correspondence between the observor's classifications and the participants' perceptions.

Hermann (1972) found that although there was some similarity in the classification of his simulated situations by the participants and the observers (experimenters), the findings as to the effects of the three attributes differed substantially according to whether the participants' or observers' classifications were used. In the present study, as we have just noted, it was feasible to employ only observer (i.e., the author's) classifications. It should be borne in mind that the results might be somewhat different if it had been possible to use the participants' perceptions instead.

3. The alternative operationalization also turned out to have greater explanatory power than Hermann's. See note 19 for comparative data.

4. My own judgment on the basis of familiarity with the cases indicated this would discriminate fairly well among the cases and also be a feasible cutoff point. That is, cases tended to be considerably less than or more than six months, with few marginal cases around six months.

5. In the Hermann (1972) simulation studies, decision time was operationalized only in terms of clock time—whether fifteen or twenty minutes—before a situation would be "significantly altered."

6. Again, familiarity with the cases suggested that such a time span would discriminate among cases and also be feasible in the sense that there would be few marginal cases.

7. Decision time is thus analytically distinct from the *duration* of situations since the latter refers to the amount of time that actually elapses between the initial and terminal points of a given situation. They are also unrelated empirically in the 65 cases since their point biserial correlation coefficient is only .06.

8. These categories are similar to those in Almond (1960) and in Deutsch et al. (1967).

9. McClelland (1968) and Brams (1969) have used the *New York Times Index* for related purposes—the former to observe international (systemic) interactions in the Berlin crisis, and the latter to measure international transactions such as diplomatic consultations.

10. The correlations (product-moment r) between the number of participant acts (level of participation) and the number of participants (scope) across the 65 cases were as follows: all types of participants (except communications) together, .95; executive branch participants, .85; congressional participants, .97; and all others (except communications), .89.

11. These conflict and consensus-building interactions are the focus of the "pluralist" model of American policy-making. See especially Hilsman (1959, 1967), Hoffmann (1968), and Huntington (1961).

12. It is not claimed that these are the only phenomena worth explaining; other focuses of attention are the effects of those outputs (Hoffman, 1968: xvii) and the nature of the international system or one of its subsystems. Scheingold (1971) has suggested that research on the North Atlantic area has neglected policy outputs.

13. For definitions and illustrations of the categories, see Fitzsimmons et al. (1969: 12 ff.).

14. The former included: M. Beloff (1963), N. Beloff (1963), Camps (1964, 1966), Cottrell and Dougherty (1964), Kitzinger (1963), Moore (1958), Schmitt (1962), and Zurcher (1958).

15. One case continued into the first month of the Nixon administration.

16. Except for 4 of the variables, the sample for the reliability tests consisted of the 115 participant acts from a randomly drawn sample of 5 cases. For 4 variables, there were too few of these 115 participants that contained relevant attributes to provide useful comparisons of the codings. Hence, for those 4 variables, a second set of 5 cases with 131 participant acts was added to the first set—for a total of 10 cases and 246 participant acts.

17. The open and public nature of the foreign policy process is discussed in Hoffmann (1968: 314-315). Hilsman (1971: 110) discusses the prestige press as an interelite communications channel. Cohen (1963: 209-215) found substantial evidence of the importance of the *New York Times* in particular.

18. Brams (1969), Azar (1970), and others have found that the *Times* coverage is not very comprehensive or typical for the activities of some countries and regions—e.g., the Middle East. But these limitations do not apply for the present data since they concern only American actors.

19. Several points about these measures of total effects should be noted. First, they refer only to the second-order interaction effects—i.e., the *combinations* of the three dichotomized variables. Additive effects—i.e., the effects of each of the three variables operating separately—are not included. A separate analysis was conducted in which both additive and interaction effects were taken into account, but yielded only very slightly higher (an average of .03) proportions of variance explained than the interaction-only results reported in this paper. Since Hermann (1969a: 30, 1970) explicitly formulates the typology only in terms of interaction effects and since the inclusion of the additive effects yields only a slightly more powerful model, the model employing only interaction effects is reported here. For discussions of additive and interaction effects in statistical analyses, see Alker (1966, 1969).

Second, the correlation ratio does not assume a linear relationship between the situational categories on the one hand and each of the dependent variables on the other; it allows for curvilinear relationships. To the extent that relationships are curvilinear, the correlation ratios (E^2) will be higher than the multiple correlation coefficient squared (R^2), since the latter does assume a linear relationship. Further analysis of the data, however, revealed that the E^2 and R^2 for each dependent variable were nearly always the same. Hence, the reported E^2 can be thought of, alternately, as R^2 in a linear regression with dummy variables. See Blalock (1960: 314 ff.) on tests for linearity and Suits (1957) on the use of dummy variables.

Third, since the primary interest here is in correlations rather than levels of statistical significance and since E is directly comparable to product-moment correlations, I have used E rather than ϵ for the correlation ratio. Although ϵ tends to be smaller than E, it would not substantially alter the findings based on E reported here. For a discussion of E and ϵ, see Blalock (1960: 267, 315-317).

Fourth, there were two different threat scores constructed on the basis of the number of the rational decision theory dimensions along which a case ranked high. For one threat score, a case was classified as a high threat situation only if it ranked high along all three of the above dimensions. For the second, it was classified high if it ranked high on two or three of the dimensions. In addition, each case was also classified according to the Hermann criteria. Thus, each case was given three different ratings—one based on the four Hermann criteria, and two based on my three operationalized dimensions derived from classical decision theory.

These indicators of threat were distinct, not only definitionally and conceptually, but also empirically for 65 cases. Comparisons of the classifications of the 65 cases for each of the three indicators showed that 21 (32%) of the cases were given different scores by the first and second indicators; 30 (46%) by the first and third; and 19 (29%) by the second and third. Both criteria for determining the explanatory power of the three revealed that the third index—i.e., a high score on all three dimensions based on the classical rational model—had the greatest explanatory power, and it is the one incorporated in the analyses reported throughout the study. Both criteria were based on the correlation ratio (E^2) between all situation types represented in the study and the clusters of dependent variables. A comparison of the correlation ratios indicated that the third index was more frequently higher. While it had the highest correlation ratio of the three indicators for 50 (not counting ties) of the 92 dependent variables in a preliminary analysis, the first index ranked first for 22 and the second for only 8. Further, the average percentage of variance explained (E^2) by the typology using the third index was the greatest. Whereas it explained an average of 11% of the variance in the 92 variables, typologies employing the first and second indicators explained only 8% and 6%, respectively.

On the other hand, there was enough similarity in the classifications to provide some reassurance of the reliability and validity of all the measures of threat, since the same scores were obtained for each pair of the three indicators in 68%, 54%, and 71% of the cases.

20. The levels of statistical significance for the differences in means are based on t-tests, and those for the correlation ratios on an analysis of variance. All significance levels referring to the variable *any action* are based on chi-squares. The actual mean scores for all the dependent variables according to situation type are located in Appendix II.

Although there may be some ambiguity as to the meaning of tests of significance when there is no random sample, there is no doubt about the fact that their size (and hence the statistical—but not necessarily theoretical—significance) depends directly on the *size of the sample*. Consequently, a difference of means or a correlation coefficient of given magnitude may be found to be statistically significant for a large sample, but statistically insignificant for a smaller sample. Since the 65 cases of this study constitute a relatively small sample by the standards of tests of statistical significance, it is not surprising that the correlations are frequently not significant at the .05 level.

21. An additional methodological problem needs brief attention—namely, controlling for the effects of variables that are extraneous to the central concerns of the study. There are two such variables that one would expect to be problematic in this

regard. One is the *duration* of each case—that is, the length of time between the initial and terminal points. One would expect the frequency of occurrence of participant acts, and thus each of the dependent variables, to be rather strongly correlated with the duration of the cases. In fact, however, this was not the case; for no dependent variable was correlated as strongly as .30 with duration; and most were less than .10. Furthermore, duration was not strongly correlated with any of the independent variables; there was no independent variable correlated (point biserial r) more than .24 with duration. Since one needs to control for the effects of an extraneous variable only if it is correlated rather strongly (i.e., in the area of .70 or higher) with both independent and dependent variables, there was clearly no need to do so for duration.

Nor was it necessary to control for the changes in participants over time. Since it clearly would not be feasible to determine the extent to which changes in all categories of participants over time are related to each independent variable (since we could not keep a record of the changes of every participant in every position), we must rely on the results of the one test that was feasible—one that provides an approximation of the relationship between changes in executive branch participants and the independent variables. It does so by classifying each case according to whether it occurred during the Truman, Eisenhower, Kennedy, or Johnson administrations, and then determining the extent to which such a classification of the cases is correlated with the situation and context attributes. Computations based on such a classification—and on a classification in which the Kennedy and Johnson categories were collapsed into a single administration (in view of the considerable continuity of high-level officials)—revealed that such changes were not strongly related to the independent variables. Specifically, no independent variable was correlated with changes in the administration more highly than .33 (as measured by the contingency coefficient C).

22. Hermann (1969b: 417) uses one of these cases (the withdrawal of the French Mediterranean fleet) as an illustration of this situation type, a slightly reassuring indication of the reliability of the coding.

23. This case is offered for *illustrative* purposes, not as documentation of the findings. It has been selected from among the others of its type on the basis of the author's judgment that it would best illustrate the attributes of inertia cases summarized above. The same applies to all of the subsequent illustrative cases.

24. The letter was later declassified and published in connection with congressional hearings (U.S. Congress, 1966: part 7, 230 f.). In those hearings, Christian Herter, who at the time was Undersecretary of State, gave a brief account of the U.S. response (1966: part 2, 41 f.).

25. Two points about the classification of the cases should be recalled here. The first is that the cases are classified according to the three situational attributes, not according to the name of the situation types. Thus, while many of these cases may not seem very "routine," they do nevertheless have the situational attributes of routine cases—namely, relatively low threat, extended decision time, and anticipation. Second, each case is classified according to the degree of threat, time, and surprise relative to the other cases. Thus, while many of these cases do not seem to be very close to a truly routine situation involving, for example, very low threat, they are nevertheless substantially closer to the corner of the "situational cube" representing those attributes than are the other cases.

26. Such a possibility seems implicit in the Hermann formulation since he mentions Chinese membership in the UN as an example of this type of situation.

27. Given the Hermann expectation of two different patterns among routine cases, it seemed appropriate to try to divide further the set of 42 routine cases along the lines indicated by the citation above. There, it will be recalled, he suggests that if a situation either has a precedent or is the occasion for interagency conflict, it would likely fall into a pattern in which the probability of positive decision is low; otherwise it would be of a type in which "execution of the recommended course of action follows prompt agreement unless temporary delays develop because policy-makers, whose approval is required, are engaged in more urgent business" (Hermann, 1969b: 419). Since we have no direct measure of interagency conflict, any attempt to further subdivide the 42 cases along these lines must be regarded as tentative. Two such attempts were made.

The first was accomplished by using the number of agencies recorded as being active as an indirect measure of interagency conflict—the assumption being that the larger the number of agencies, the greater the likelihood of conflict among them. Thus, for this classification, any case for which there was a precedent or which showed more than the mean agency score of 2.0 agencies active was classified as the second type of routine case in which action would presumably be less likely than in the first type. This criterion yielded 16 cases of the first type and 26 of the second. But a comparison of the actions-taken scores showed the comparative effects of the two types to be the opposite of the prediction. In 13% of the cases of the first type and 41% of the second type, there was some action. And there was an average of only 0.1 actions for the first type, but 0.7 for the second. Given the tenuous method of classification, though, these findings do not seem very conclusive.

The second attempt to subdivide the 42 cases was based only on the criterion of whether or not there was a precedent for each case. This second attempt produced 28 cases that fall into the first pattern described above and 14 cases of the second type. In this case, action was in fact slightly more common for the first type, as predicted, but again the data must be regarded as rather inconclusive. In 32% of the cases of the first type, there was some action—and an average of 0.5 actions per case; in 28% of the second type, there was some action—and an average of 0.4 actions per case. Other kinds of outputs by executive branch participants were also slightly more common among the cases of the first type—as were participation levels for most types of elites. But the differences were quite small; and, moreover, there was no pattern in the differences along the intellective and political dimensions of the process. Hence, we must conclude that, while there is some evidence to support the differences hypothesized by Hermann, the evidence is mixed and generally inconclusive.

28. I am using the terms *explanatory power* and *explanation* in the sense of correlations among variables—a usage that is not inconsistent with other modes of explanation such as functional or analogical theories. For a brief discussion of these and other modes of explanation commonly used in international political analysis, see Coplin and Kegley (1971: 417 f.).

29. Karl Deutsch has allowed that "Anyone who suggests a variable explaining an additional 10% of the variance has made a contribution to political theory" (quoted in Alker, 1965: 89). See also Rosenau (1968: 216 n.).

30. There is a technical statistical point that should also be taken into account. When the variance in a variable is quite small, there is an inherent depressant effect on the size of any correlation involving that variable. It will be recalled that the range for attention to feedback was only 0 to 3.

31. These tests were based on a collapsed matrix of three comparisons rather than five for all five types of issues—a reduction necessitated by small expected frequencies in the full matrix. Thus, reflexive and deliberative cases were collapsed into one type and administrative and routine cases into another—on the assumption that the former were the two highest categories and the latter the two moderate or middle categories in terms of whether any action was taken.

REFERENCES

ALKER, H. R., Jr. (1969) "Statistics and politics: the need for causal data analysis," in S. M. Lipset (ed.) Politics and the Social Sciences. New York: Oxford Univ. Press.
--- (1966) "The long road to international relations theory: problems of statistical nonadditivity." World Politics 23.
--- (1965) Mathematics and Politics. New York: Macmillan.
ALMOND, G. A. (1960) The American People and Foreign Policy. New York: Frederick A. Praeger.
AZAR, E. E. (1970) "Analysis of international events." Peace Research Reviews 4 (November).
BELOFF, M. (1963) The United States and the Unity of Europe. New York: Vintage.
BELOFF, N. (1963) The General Says No. Baltimore: Penguin.
BLALOCK, H. M. (1960) Social Statistics. New York: McGraw-Hill.
BRAMS, S. J. (1969) "The structure of influence relationships in the international system," in J. N. Rosenau (ed.) International Politics and Foreign Policy. New York: Free Press.
BREWER, T. L. (1971) "Issue type and context in American foreign policy-making: an analysis of elite behavior in sixty-five European integration and Atlantic alliance cases, 1949-1968." Ph.D. dissertation. State University of New York at Buffalo.
--- (forthcoming a) "Foreign policy process events: problems of concept and data," in E. E. Azar and J. Ben Dak (eds.) International Interactions.
--- (forthcoming b) "Issue type and context in foreign policy-making: effects on American elite behavior."
CAMPS, M. (1966) European Unification in the Sixties: From the Veto to the Crisis. New York: McGraw Hill.
--- (1964) Britain and the European Community, 1955-1963. Princeton, N.J.: Princeton Univ. Press.
COHEN, B. C. (1967) "Mass communication and foreign policy," in J. N. Rosenau (ed.) Domestic Sources of Foreign Policy. New York: Free Press.
--- (1963) The Press and Foreign Policy. Princeton, N.J.: Princeton Univ. Press.
COPLIN, W. D. and C. W. KEGLEY, Jr. (1971) A Multi-Method Introduction to International Politics. Chicago: Markham.
COTTRELL, A. J. and J. E. DOUGHERTY (1964) The Politics of the Atlantic Alliance. New York: Frederick A. Praeger.
DEUTSCH, K. W. (1963) The Nerves of Government. New York: Free Press.
--- L. J. EDINGER, R. C. MACRIDIS, and R. L. MERRITT (1967) France, Germany and the Western Alliance. New York: Charles Scribner's.
EASTON, D. (1965) A Systems Analysis of Political Life. New York: John Wiley.

EDWARDS, W. (1954) "The theory of decision-making." Psych. Bull. 51.

FITZSIMMONS, B., G. HOGGARD, C. McCLELLAND, W. MARTIN, and R. YOUNG (1969) "World event/interaction survey handbook and codebook." Univ. of Southern California. (mimeo)

GAMSON, W. A. and A. MODIGLIANI (1971) Untangling the Cold War. Boston: Little, Brown.

GEORGE, A. L. (1955) "American policy-making and the North Korean aggression." World Politics 7.

HERMANN, C. F. (1972) "Threat, time and surprise," in International Crises. New York: Free Press.

--- (1969a) Crises in Foreign Policy. Indianapolis, Ind.: Bobbs-Merrill.

--- (1969b) "International crisis as a situational variable," in J. N. Rosenau (ed.) International Politics and Foreign Policy. New York: Free Press.

--- (1963) "Some consequences of crisis which limit the viability of organizations." Administrative Sci. Q. 8 (June).

HILSMAN, R. (1971) The Politics of Policy Making in Defense and Foreign Affairs. New York: Harper & Row.

--- (1967) To Move a Nation. New York: Dell.

--- (1959) "The foreign policy consensus." J. of Conflict Resolution, 3.

HOFFMAN, S. (1968) Gulliver's Troubles, Or the Setting of American Foreign Policy. New York: McGraw-Hill.

HOLSTI, O. R. (1967) "Cognitive dynamics and images of the enemy." J. of International Affairs 21.

--- (1962) "The belief system and national images." J. of Conflict Resolution 6.

HUNTINGTON, S. P. (1961) The Common Defense. New York: Columbia Univ. Press.

KITZINGER, U. W. (1963) The Politics and Economics of European Integration. New York: Frederick A. Praeger.

McCLELLAND, C. A. (1968) "Access to Berlin: the quantity and variety of events, 1948-1963," in J. D. Singer (ed.) Quantitative International Politics. New York: Free Press.

MOORE, B. T. (1958) NATO and the Future of Europe. New York: Harper.

RANNEY, A. (1968) "The study of policy content," in Political Science and Public Policy. Chicago: Markham.

ROBINSON, J. A. (1968) "Crisis," in D. L. Sills (ed.) International Encyclopedia of the Social Sciences. New York: Macmillan and Free Press.

--- and R. C. SNYDER (1965) "Decision-making in international politics," in H. C. Kelman (ed.) International Political Behavior. New York: Holt, Rinehart & Winston.

ROBINSON, J. A., C. F. HERMANN, and M. G. HERMANN (1969) "Search under crisis in political gaming and simulation," in D. G. Pruitt and R. C. Snyder (eds.) Theory and Research on the Causes of War. Englewood Cliffs, N.J.: Prentice-Hall.

ROBINSON, W. S. (1957) "The statistical measure of agreement." Amer. Soc. Rev. 22.

ROSENAU, J. N. (1968) "Private preferences and political responsibilities," in J. D. Singer (ed.) Quantitative International Politics. New York: Free Press.

SCHEINGOLD, S. A. (1971) "The North Atlantic area as a policy arena." International Studies Q. 15.

SCHMITT, H. A. (1962) The Path to European Union. Baton Rouge, La.: Louisiana State Univ. Press.

SUITS, D. B. (1957) "Use of dummy variables in regression equations." J. of Amer. Statistical Assn. 52.

TAYLOR, D. W. (1965) "Decision making and problem solving," in J. G. March (ed.) Handbook of Organizations. Chicago: Rand McNally.

TINBERGEN, J. and H. C. BOS (1962) Mathematical Models of Economic Growth. New York: McGraw-Hill.

U.S. Congress (1966) "The Atlantic Alliance." Hearings of the Subcommittee on National Security and International Operations of the Committee on Government Operations, April 27-August 15.

VAN DYKE, V. (1968) "Process and policy as focal concepts in political research," in A. Ranney (ed.) Political Science and Public Policy. Chicago: Markham.

ZURCHER, A. J. (1958) The Struggle to Unite Europe, 1940-1958. New York: New York Univ. Press.

THOMAS L. BREWER was born in Indianapolis, Indiana, in 1941. He received his undergraduate education at Wabash College, his M.A. in International Relations from Yale University, and his Ph.D. in Political Science from the State University of New York at Buffalo. His publications include "Elite Orientations toward the European and Atlantic Communities," in The General Inquirer *(1966)*, and "Foreign Policy Process Events," in International Interactions *(forthcoming)*. He is spending the 1972-1973 academic year at the George Washington University, School of Public and International Affairs, Naval War College Center, in Newport, Rhode Island. He is on leave from the faculty of Eastern Michigan University.